praise for nicole hunn

"Hunn has not only bestowed her readers with a complete cookbook...but she shows us how to save money, and time, on our meals...It's well worth a bite."
—San Francisco Book Review

"Even when she's telling you something you think you already know—like grow your own vegetables—Hunn adds an extra bit of information that takes the wisdom to another level."
—Epicurious.com

"No childhood favorites are off-limits with *Gluten-Free Classic Snacks* by author/blogger Nicole Hunn of *Gluten-Free on a Shoestring*. Expect recipe riffs on Twinkies, Thin Mints, Nutter Butters, Pop Tarts and more in her ode to edible Americana."
—GFF Magazine

"Nicole Hunn serves up all the recipes and information found in her cookbook in the friendly and inviting manner that has helped make her blog popular."
—National Foundation for Celiac Awareness

"Hunn is clever and optimistic. As you flip through the pages, it's hard to avoid not feeling better about your gluten-free life. Plus, the recipes will inspire you to go into the kitchen with renewed energy and hope for the future. It's well worth spending money to purchase *Gluten-Free on a Shoestring*. It will pay dividends in the future."
—Gluten-Free Living

"I highly recommend [*Gluten-Free on a Shoestring Quick & Easy*]. The recipes are accessible and especially geared for people with busy lifestyles."
—Tucson Citizen

"Hunn has assembled 125 recipes that say 'make me, make me!,' and all the reader need do is pick where to start...It is a user-friendly cookbook with satisfying recipes that are easy to prepare. Saving money is the icing on the (gluten-free) cake."
—Technorati.com

"Hunn successfully tackles a chief complaint voiced by special-diet newbies: sticker shock. Her practical tips for shopping and cooking to save time and money are a gift to all of us who are paying too much for too little."
—Living Without

"Compiles [Hunn's] best recipes and helpful hints on cutting costs, all in best friend blogger-style. Her tips to economizing are good reminders and handy for the working parent."
—Marin Independent Journal

"Opens up a whole new world for people with this particular diet restriction and does so with a writing style that is both assured and accessible. Those of us who don't have a medical diagnosis requiring diet changes can benefit from the book, as well...In addition to offering an excellent resource for those who must go gluten-free, Hunn's book gives everyone a map toward healthier eating without giving up those delicious foods we love."
—Curled Up With a Good Book

"From locating best values to meal planning and stocking a gluten-free pantry, this provides a range of foods from 'scratch' that can fit any budget. Highly recommended!"
—Midwest Book Review

"This book is written for real people, facing real economic issues, that can't afford to dedicate a whole paycheck to groceries. It is a great resource for preparing whole foods at home and not spending all weekends and evenings in the kitchen."
—Portland Book Review

gluten-free
small bites

ALSO BY NICOLE HUNN

Gluten-Free on a Shoestring

Gluten-Free on a Shoestring Quick & Easy

Gluten-Free on a Shoestring Bakes Bread

Gluten-Free Classic Snacks

gluten-free small bites

sweet and savory handheld
treats for on-the-go lifestyles
and entertaining

❦

NICOLE HUNN

Photographs by Jennifer May

❦

Da Capo
∞
LIFE
LONG

Da Capo Lifelong Books

Copyright © 2016 by Nicole Hunn
Photographs by Jennifer May
All rights reserved. No part of this publication may be reproduced, stored in a retrieval system, or transmitted, in any form or by any means, electronic, mechanical, photocopying, recording, or otherwise, without the prior written permission of the publisher. Printed in the United States of America. For information, address Da Capo Press, 44 Farnsworth Street, 3rd Floor, Boston, MA 02210.

Designed by Lisa Diercks / Endpaper Studio
Set in Neutraface No. 2

Cataloging-in-Publication data for this book is available from the Library of Congress.
First Da Capo Press edition 2016
ISBN: 978-0-7382-1858-8 (paperback)
ISBN: 978-0-7382-1922-6 (e-book)

Published by Da Capo Press, an imprint of Perseus Books, LLC, a subsidiary of Hachette Book Group, Inc.

www.dacapopress.com

NOTE: The information in this book is true and complete to the best of our knowledge. This book is intended only as an informative guide for those wishing to know more about health issues. In no way is this book intended to replace, countermand, or conflict with the advice given to you by your own physician. The ultimate decision concerning care should be made between you and your doctor. We strongly recommend you follow his or her advice. Information in this book is general and is offered with no guarantees on the part of the authors or Da Capo Press. The authors and publisher disclaim all liability in connection with the use of this book.

Da Capo Press books are available at special discounts for bulk purchases in the U.S. by corporations, institutions, and other organizations. For more information, please contact the Special Markets Department at the Perseus Books Group, 2300 Chestnut Street, Suite 200, Philadelphia, PA 19103, or call (800) 810-4145, ext. 5000, or e-mail special.markets@perseusbooks.com.

10 9 8 7 6 5 4 3 2 1

contents

introduction:
small bites, big flavor

Ideally, we all eat three square meals a day, every day—no sweets, no snacks, no buttery delicacies for which we might feel guilty the next day. We all sit down to a quiet meal every evening, where the only gentle distraction is some pleasant conversation among dining companions. When we have guests, we break out the tablecloth and napkin rings, begin with a soup or salad, and move on to an elaborate main course. And everyone is content with one slice of cake for dessert. We don't ply our children with snacks in the car, or after the game, no sir. We eat early in the morning but never late at night. And we never *ever* eat on the run.

And then we wake up. We remember that variety is the spice of life and that finger foods are just where it's at sometimes. We live in the real world, where pigs in blankets are the first appetizers to disappear at any affair for good reason (they're *delicious*). We're rushing around from one meeting to another, one sporting event to the next, or from the doctor's office to our offices. Sometimes, you just need a snack to get through to the next meal and there's no reason not to enjoy it, even if you're eating it in your car. Other times, dinner itself is handheld so some can eat it at the table, others on the go.

When you think of small bites, do you just think of fancy parties with butler-passed hors d'oeuvres (and no small children in sight)? If that's what you're after, these recipes can certainly be served on fancy silver trays by white-gloved waitstaff. But if the closest you come to a staff is when your dog cleans up the floor after a spill in the kitchen, you'll find yourself quite at home here. Small bites are the party foods that you break out when you're hosting the book club, and the mini quiches you bring to a potluck. They're the handheld chicken potpies you know your children can devour in the back of the car on the way from the dentist or ballet class or basketball practice. They're also the mini sweets no one can resist, since in a bite or two . . . they're gone!

I'll start you off with the basics—tools, ingredients, tricks, and my tips for top-notch flour blends. And then . . . the recipes. The first recipe chapter is everyone's favorite—deliciously fried foods. Everything from crab Rangoon and potato croquettes to cheese puffs and samosas. (You'll find no-fry alternatives, too, for nearly every recipe that calls for frying, just in case I don't succeed in convincing you that deep-frying is a glorious thing). Next up are hearty meat-based snacks, like buffalo chicken meatballs, pretzel dogs, and miniature chicken and waffles (yes, you did just read that). Not feeling the meat? Vegetarian bites bring back favorites like stuffed mushrooms and spinach balls, fried green tomatoes and jalapeño poppers. There's a chapter devoted to bigger bites: wraps and roll-ups that give boring old sandwiches a run for their money, with spring rolls, taquitos, and cheesesteak wraps. There's even a whole chapter on dinner to go, with handheld foods like miniature shepherd's pies, chicken potpies, and empanadas (and of course you can eat them for lunch or even breakfast, if that's your thing). Sweet Endings pack all the chewy, crunchy, chocolaty taste of dessert into everything from mini éclairs and mini apple pies to crispy cookie chips and petit fours.

What would a *Gluten-Free on a Shoestring* book be without a chapter devoted to staples—all the recipes for wraps and doughs that you need to make all your favorite small bites? You'll be surprised how good you'll get at cranking out gluten-free flour tortillas and soft tacos in your own kitchen, then freezing them in batches for when you really need them.

The foods you make with these recipes will all be gone in just a few (small) bites. But for those times when the whole family magically appears at home for dinner, there are suggestions, throughout the book, on how to make the recipes in bigger bites for a more leisurely meal—plus suggestions for how to freeze and make-ahead portions of each recipe.

For some fun extras to go along with your purchase of this book, please visit this special page on the web: http://glutenfreeonashoestring.com/smallbites. Remember, life is sweet and fun. Gluten is expendable.

With love,
Nicole

chapter 1: the basics

Gluten-Free Flour Blends

GENERAL GUIDELINES

In gluten-free baking, no one individual flour can serve as an all-purpose flour, one that functions largely the same as conventional gluten-containing all-purpose flour. Instead, we rely upon a blend of flours that together are good for "all purposes." Just like flours in conventional baking, no one blend is ideal for every unique purpose. A pastry flour is low in protein and high in starch, for a certain lightness and comparative lack of chew. Bread flour is essentially the opposite: low starch, high protein for flexibility and chew. So it goes in gluten-free baking as well. You can either purchase an all-purpose gluten-free flour, already blended, or blend your own for use in every recipe in this cookbook that calls for an all-purpose gluten-free flour (which is most of the recipes in this book). If you would like to purchase a ready-made all-purpose gluten-free flour blend, I discuss below the two I recommend. If you would prefer to blend your own, there are recipes on page 4 for you to do just that, along with any additional information you may need about some of the component flours.

When a recipe in this cookbook calls for an "all-purpose gluten-free flour," the blend must contain xanthan gum. When a recipe calls specifically for the Basic Gum-Free Gluten-Free Flour blend, only the specific amount of xanthan gum indicated, if any, as a separate ingredient in the recipe, is appropriate. Those recipes require a lower xanthan gum proportion than other recipes, or none at all, and use of an all-purpose gluten-free flour blend that already contains xanthan gum will lead to a poor result.

COMMERCIALLY AVAILABLE ALL-PURPOSE GLUTEN-FREE FLOURS

Better Batter and Cup4Cup. These are my two favorite brands of commercially available all-purpose gluten-free flour blends. The two all-purpose gluten-free flour blend recipes I provide are a Mock Better Batter Gluten-Free Flour, which approximates the results achieved with Better Batter Gluten-Free Flour, and my Better Than Cup4Cup Gluten-Free Flour, which corrects what I think is an imbalance in Cup4Cup itself. Either of those blends can be used successfully in any recipe in this book that calls for an all-purpose gluten-free flour.

Better Batter Gluten-Free Flour is the one true all-purpose gluten-free flour that I have used most consistently since 2009. It is a well-balanced blend of superfine white rice flour, superfine brown rice flour, tapioca starch, potato starch, potato flour, xanthan gum, and pectin. I always order it directly from the company itself through the website, betterbatter.org, as that is the best price; I find it cheaper (and of course more convenient) to purchase it than to build my own with individual flours.

Cup4Cup gluten-free flour really works best as a pastry flour or a cake flour, as it is quite high in starch, and I don't recommend it for recipes in this book as a substitute for all-purpose gluten-free flour.

Cup4Cup as cake flour. If you do decide to use Cup4Cup in any of the recipes in this book as an all-purpose gluten-free flour, if that recipe also calls for cornstarch, please use more Cup4Cup, gram for gram, in place of the cornstarch. Therefore, if a recipe calls for 100 grams of all-purpose gluten-free flour and 10 grams of cornstarch, if you are using Cup4Cup as the all-purpose gluten-free flour, instead use 110 grams Cup4Cup.

HOMEMADE GLUTEN-FREE FLOUR BLENDS AND SPECIALTY GLUTEN-FREE FLOUR BLENDS

We begin our discussion of these homemade flour blends with some information about the individual ingredients. I promise this isn't a science lesson! It's just enough information to help you feel comfortable with each component.

Expandex modified tapioca starch. Expandex brand modified tapioca starch is a chemically (not genetically!) modified tapioca starch that, in small amounts and in the proper recipe, gives gluten-free baked goods an elasticity that can't be achieved otherwise. I first introduced this incredibly useful ingredient in *Gluten-Free on a Shoestring Bakes Bread*, and it remains irreplaceable in building my gluten-free bread flour blend (see page 4). In certain, limited instances, however, Expandex can be replaced with plain tapioca starch/flour, gram for gram. In this book, I have indicated that the substitution is a possibility in the recipes themselves. For additional information on where to buy Expandex modified tapioca starch (including information on how to use Ultratex 3, another type of modified tapioca starch, in place of Expandex in the bread flour; Ultratex 3 is more widely available online worldwide and is approximately three times as strong as Expandex), please see the Resources page on my blog: http://glutenfreeonashoestring.com/gluten-free-resources.

Gluten-free bread flour. To build the bread flour blend, I use NOW Brand unflavored whey protein isolate (which is nearly all protein—you must use isolate, not whey powder or whey protein concentrate), which I purchase online through vitacost.com or amazon.com, depending upon which site has the best price at that time.

Potato flour. Potato flour is made from whole potatoes that are dried and then ground into flour. It is very useful in gluten-free baking as it helps to hold baked goods together. There really is no substitute for its particular baking qualities.

Potato starch. Potato starch is made from dehydrated potatoes that have been peeled. It adds lightness to baked goods. It's a very different ingredient from potato flour, and they are not at all interchangeable. Cornstarch or arrowroot can often be substituted for potato starch.

Pure powdered pectin. The powdered pectin you use must be only pure pectin, which contains no other additives (like glucose and other sugars). I buy pectin directly from Pomona Pectin (www.pomonapectin.com). You use only the pectin, not the calcium packet.

Rice flours. Please note that, to build an all-purpose gluten-free flour successfully, you *must* use a digital kitchen scale (page 9), and you *must* use superfine rice flours as all other rice flours will have a gritty taste. The only source I know of for truly superfine rice flours is Authentic Foods. Authentic Foods superfine brown rice flour and superfine white rice flour are sold on amazon.com, on the Authentic Foods website, and also in some select brick-and-mortar stores but often for a higher price than you can find online. Vitacost.com has also started marketing its own superfine white rice flour, and although it is not truly as superfine as Authentic Foods' brand, it certainly has a finer grain than most.

Tapioca starch/flour. This starch/flour should be purchased from either nuts.com or Authentic Foods for consistent quality. Bob's Red Mill Tapioca Flour is of very inconsistent quality, as are many other brands. I must also caution against buying any component flours from Asian food stores, as they are often contaminated with gluten-containing grains both before reaching the store and in the store itself and may contain other additives.

Xanthan gum. In gluten-free baking, xanthan gum is a plant-based thickening and stabilizing agent that helps to give batter and dough elasticity and thickness. When a recipe calls for an all-purpose gluten-free flour, the flour blend will already contain a specific amount of xanthan gum. When a recipe calls specifically for the Basic Gum-Free Gluten-Free Flour blend, however, you'll be adding xanthan gum separately in an amount lower than what would be included in an all-purpose blend, or eliminating it as an ingredient altogether as instructed in the individual recipe.

THE HOMEMADE FLOUR BLENDS

All the flour blend recipes that follow can be multiplied by as many factors as you like. I typically make at least 10 cups at a time by just multiplying every ingredient by 10, placing the ingredients in a large, airtight, lidded container, and whisking very well. For an online calculator that does the math for you, please see the page "Flour Blends" on my website: http://glutenfreeonashoestring.com/all-purpose-gluten-free-flour-recipes/.

1 cup (140 g) Mock Better Batter All-Purpose Gluten-Free Flour

42 grams (about ¼ cup) superfine white rice flour (30%)
42 grams (about ¼ cup) superfine brown rice flour (30%)
21 grams (about 2⅓ tablespoons) tapioca starch/flour (15%)
21 grams (about 2⅓ tablespoons) potato starch (15%)
7 grams (about 1¾ teaspoons) potato flour (5%)
4 grams (about 2 teaspoons) xanthan gum (3%)
3 grams (about 1½ teaspoons) pure powdered fruit pectin (2%)

1 cup (140 g) Better Than Cup4Cup All-Purpose Gluten-Free Flour

42 grams (about ¼ cup) superfine white rice flour (30%)
25 grams (about 8⅓ teaspoons) cornstarch (18%)
24 grams (about 2½ tablespoons) superfine brown rice flour (17%)
21 grams (about 2⅓ tablespoons) tapioca starch/flour (15%)
21 grams (about 3⅓ tablespoons, before grinding) nonfat dry milk, ground into a finer powder (15%)
4 grams (about 1 teaspoon) potato starch (3%)
3 grams (about 1½ teaspoons) xanthan gum (2%)

1 cup (140 g) Basic Gum-Free Gluten-Free Flour

93 grams (about 9⅓ tablespoons) superfine white rice flour (66%)
32 grams (about 3½ tablespoons) potato starch (23%)
15 grams (about 5 teaspoons) tapioca starch/flour (11%)

1 cup (140 g) Gluten-Free Bread Flour

100 grams (about 11½ tablespoons) Mock Better Batter All-Purpose Gluten-Free Flour (71%)
25 grams (about 5 tablespoons) unflavored whey protein isolate (18%)
15 grams (about 5 teaspoons) Expandex modified tapioca starch (11%)

1 cup (140 g) Gluten-Free Pastry Flour

112 grams (about 13 tablespoons) Mock Better Batter All-Purpose Gluten-Free Flour (80%)
14 grams (about 2⅔ tablespoons) nonfat dry milk, ground into a finer powder (10%)
14 grams (about 1½ tablespoons) cornstarch (10%)

Note that my Better Than Cup4Cup All-Purpose Gluten-Free Flour or Cup4Cup Gluten-Free Flour itself can be used in place of Gluten-Free Pastry Flour, gram for gram.

Deep-Frying

DON'T FEAR THE DEEP-FRY

There are plenty of recipes in this book that call for deep-frying. You probably have some mixed feelings about that. I get it. Cooking your food in three inches of oil is not generally anyone's idea of health food. And although deep-frying is the only way to get that authentic egg roll (page 35) or jalapeño popper (page 17) taste, whenever possible I have included instructions in each recipe for a no-fry option. That being said, indulge me for a moment while I sing the praises of deep-frying:

1. Deep-frying food is not as unhealthy as it's generally considered. When food is deep fried at the proper temperature, the outside of the dough is sealed quickly, preventing any more oil from being absorbed and allowing the hot oil to gently cook the inside. Shallow frying causes food to absorb oil the entire time.

2. Deep-frying doesn't heat up the house like turning on the oven does. Perfect for those warm weather months, and for those times when your oven is already busy.

3. It's ridiculous how tender and delicious fried foods can be. You know you'll never get that egg roll to crackle when you bite into it when you bake it in the oven.

TIPS FOR SUCCESSFUL DEEP-FRYING

If I've at least convinced you to *try* deep-frying, I've got you right where I want you. Now it's time to go through the tips I've learned over the years that keep my family in deep-fried goodness.

1. Frying oil. Peanut oil and corn oil are ideal for deep-frying, as they have a neutral taste and a very high smoke point of 450°F. That means that they can get really, really hot before they start smoking. Smoking oil is more likely to catch fire and has an unpleasant taste. Rice bran oil also has a neutral taste and an even higher smoke point of 490°F. All are ideal for deep-frying. So-called vegetable oil varies in smoke point, as the components of the oil vary. It typically has at least a smoke point of over 400°F, so can be used for deep-drying as well, but the previously mentioned oils are all preferable.

2. Oil temperature. Keeping the oil at a constant temperature is really important. When you add each piece of food to the oil, it will lower the temperature slightly. The more pieces of food you add at a time, the more it will lower the oil temperature. So heat the oil to the temperature directed in the recipe, as read on an instant-read thermometer, fry in small batches, and be sure to allow the oil to reheat to temperature in between batches.

3. Food temperature. The food you place in the hot oil should be at or close to room temperature when you fry it. If it is frozen, it must be defrosted first. Otherwise, the frozen food will lower the oil temperature significantly upon contact, the food will absorb too much oil, and it will not behave as you expect.

4. Condition of frying oil. Slightly "dirty" frying oil fries more evenly and better than completely clean (virgin) frying oil. If your frying oil is fresh, try dirtying it a bit by frying a crusty bit of bread first. Or just consider your first piece of fried food the sacrificial lamb.

5. Reusing frying oil. Unless I have fried something with a strong odor, like fish, I typically use a batch of frying oil three times before I throw it away. Not only does dirty oil fry better, but it's also much more economical and less wasteful in general. After I use frying oil, I allow it to cool, and then I strain it through a fine-mesh sieve into a container, often right back into the original (now-empty) container from which the oil came. If the container has a small opening, I position a small funnel between the container and the strainer. Then, I mark the container "frying oil," and put one hash mark on the label for each time I have used the oil. After three uses, I return the oil to the container, seal it, and then throw it away. Never pour oil down your drain or you'll clog it!

6. Oil and water don't mix, for real. When frying in hot oil, water is your enemy. Even a tiny droplet of water falling into your frying oil will cause spurting and splattering. So pat wet foods dry as best you can and never ever place food in the fryer with wet hands.

Ingredient Notes

I haven't listed every single ingredient you'll need, since most of the recipes call for everyday items. But there are a few outliers that you may not have in your pantry.

Almond paste. This thick, sweet paste is made of blanched almonds, confectioners' sugar, and egg whites, processed until smooth and sticky. It's almost the same as marzipan, which has the same ingredients but a higher proportion of sugar than almond paste. Luckily, Solo brand almond paste and Love'n Bake brand almond paste are both gluten-free.

Dairy ingredients. Liquid milk, when called for as an ingredient, can be any kind, as long as it's not nonfat. When nonfat dry milk is called for as an ingredient, it is evaporated non-fat dairy milk (it is always sold as nonfat, so I use that by default). I use Carnation brand. Try replacing it with powdered coconut milk (as of the printing of this book, Native Forest brand coconut milk powder is dairy-free and gluten-free) or with finely ground almond flour in a 1:1 ratio. Dairy milk can be replaced with unsweetened almond milk, or coconut milk, and in most instances heavy whipping cream can be substituted with canned full-fat coconut milk, also in a 1:1 ratio. As a substitute for unsalted butter, I recommend using nonhydrogenated vegetable shortening, gram for gram. I use Spectrum Organic shortening, and it's made from sustainably harvested palm oil. Virgin coconut oil can be replaced with shortening gram for gram as well. Cream cheese can be replaced with nondairy cream cheese. Sour cream can be replaced with nondairy sour cream or Greek-style dairy or nondairy yogurt. For cheese, Daiya Italian shred blend nondairy cheese melts relatively well and has a nice, cheesy taste (that last part is a good thing when you're talking about cheese). For Parmigiano-Reggiano cheese in particular, try substituting nutritional yeast. It's an inactive, flaked yeast made from sugarcane and beet molasses. As vegans have long known, it has a wonderfully nutty flavor and a similar texture to grated Parm. You can find nutritional yeast online, in natural food stores, or at Whole Foods (two good brands are Bragg and Bob's Red Mill). If you've resisted trying it before but you're avoiding dairy, it might just be your new favorite ingredient.

Dried gluten-free pasta. For many years, I used Tinkyada gluten-free rice pasta almost exclusively (I also really like Sam Mills gluten-free corn pasta). Although I still occasionally buy Tinkyada (their gluten-free lasagna noodles are the best I've tried and reasonably priced), now that Barilla makes certified gluten-free pasta, I'm a convert. If Barilla makes the shape of dried pasta I'm seeking, I'll choose that over any other. It cooks al dente without any special treatment, although I usually rinse the pasta lightly with warm water after I drain it since there is just so much starch in the water.

Ghee or clarified butter. Ghee is pure butterfat and is created by removing the milk solids and water from the butter itself. It is made by melting butter for the purpose of evaporating the water and separating the milk solids, which naturally fall out when the butter is heated. Unlike clarified butter, which is made in the same manner, when making ghee, the milk solids are browned slightly during preparation. For our purposes, the two ingredients are interchangeable.

Hoisin sauce. Hoisin sauce is a thick, dark sauce used in Chinese cooking that's sweet, salty, and spicy. It's available in the Asian section of your grocery store. Sun Luck brand hoisin sauce is gluten-free. If you don't have any hoisin sauce on hand, try substituting a mixture of half gluten-free miso paste and half molasses, with a dash of rice vinegar.

Kosher salt. Kosher salt is simply salt with a semicoarse grind, and it is much harder to overmeasure than table salt. It can be substituted with lightly flaked sea salt, one for one. If you would like to substitute it with table salt, try using about half the volume, as table salt has a significantly finer grain and is therefore much more concentrated.

Masa harina corn flour. Masa harina corn flour is made from dried corn that is then cooked in limewater before being dried and ground again. It is one of my favorite gluten-free grains, as it is so versatile and useful that it can be turned into corn tortillas with the simple addition of water and salt (page 202). Maseca masa harina corn flour is gluten-free, as is Bob's Red Mill brand. Nuts.com also sells certified gluten-free masa harina.

Packaged tortillas. Chapter 5 has recipes for every sort of wrap imaginable. They all freeze quite well, and I highly recommend keeping your freezer stocked with a healthy supply. But there are those times when you're going to be caught out, unable to make them from scratch. Unfortunately, there are painfully few options for store-bought gluten-free flour tortillas. I've tried a number of them, and for the most part, they just don't cut it. They may bend, but they peel and break, too. And once you learn how good a homemade gluten-free wrap can be, it becomes very, very hard to forget. I simply cannot recommend any of them. Corn tortillas are something of a different story. There are a number of reliably gluten-free corn tortillas, among them Mission and La Banderita brands. They are serviceable, particularly if you heat them one at a time in a hot, dry cast-iron skillet. I can't lie, though. Some of my children refuse to eat them. That might be because they are food spoiled. But if I'm being honest, I kind of want you to be, too. For what it's worth, I do keep a steady supply of Mission gluten-free yellow corn tortillas in my refrigerator. Put enough cheese on anything, and my children generally will eat it.

Panko-style gluten-free breadcrumbs. Ian's Foods makes really nice packaged panko-style gluten-free breadcrumbs. I have ordered it in bulk online to have on hand. Please see page 216 for a simple recipe for homemade panko-style gluten-free breadcrumbs.

Spring roll rice wrappers. My favorite brand of spring roll wrappers, the kind that you soften in warm water before filling and shaping, is Happy Pho Vietnamese Brown Rice Spring Roll Wrappers. They're reliably gluten-free, available on amazon.com as well as in brick-and-mortar stores, and are well priced.

Tamari or gluten-free soy sauce. Tamari and soy sauce are both by-products of fermented soybeans, but soy sauce typically contains wheat and tamari does not. Tamari is a bit richer in color and flavor than soy sauce and also a bit less salty, but the two are similar enough as to be indistinguishable for our purposes. Kikkoman gluten-free soy sauce is generally my favorite brand of gluten-free soy sauce (be sure you are buying the gluten-free variety, as it's not the only one they sell). San-J brand tamari is gluten-free.

Vegetable shortening. Shortening has less moisture than butter, so baked goods made using it in place of butter tend to crisp and spread considerably less. Sometimes, a combination of butter and shortening is called for in a recipe to achieve a particular texture. For best results, always follow the recipe as it is written. If you have environmental or health concerns about using vegetable shortening, please note that I use Spectrum brand nonhydrogenated vegetable shortening, which is made from sustainable palm oil and contains no hydrogenated oils.

Storing Fresh Ingredients

For maximum shelf life of refrigerated ingredients, here are a few pointers.

Fresh asparagus. If you're anything like me, sometimes you buy asparagus with the best of intentions for making it that day or the next, and the next thing you know, you're tossing a slimy mess into the trash can. To keep fresh asparagus crisp for up to a week or more, try filling a quart-size wide-mouth canning jar or other container of similar size and shape with tap water and placing the asparagus in the jar, cut-side down. Store the jar with the asparagus in the refrigerator until you're ready to use it. Refresh the water once every couple of days. They will keep fresh and crisp for at least a week.

Fresh ginger root. Ginger can be stored in the freezer, and you'll never find yourself without it. No need to defrost or peel it before using.

Scallions. These green onions can be stored in one of two ways. Tie them together with a twist tie and place them in a tall mason jar filled about halfway with water, roots facing down. Place the jar in the refrigerator, and it will buy you at least a week. Your refrigerator may be somewhat smelly during that time, though. My preferred way of storing scallions is one that ensures I will always have some on hand. Simply wash and chop the scallions, then spread them in a single layer on a lined rimmed baking sheet. Place the baking sheet in the freezer until the scallions are frozen. Transfer them to a zip-top bag and store them in the freezer. They defrost very quickly when removed from the freezer. This method allows you to use as many or as few as you like, and once frozen, they don't have an odor at all so no worries about a smelly freezer.

Special Kitchen Equipment

Bench scraper/bowl scraper. For handling and shaping bread dough, a metal bench scraper or a plastic bowl scraper is very useful. They both perform the same function of allowing you to lift and manipulate the dough, but I generally prefer a plastic bowl scraper as it is somewhat flexible. It's also useful for its intended purpose, which is cleaning every last drop out of a mixing bowl.

Cake cutters. To make tortillas of every kind with nice, clean professional-looking edges, consider purchasing cake cutters. I have a 6-inch cake cutter and an 8-inch cake cutter, both metal and made by Fat Daddio's. I have purchased them on amazon.com and in well-stocked kitchen supply stores. The 6-inch cutter tends to be a bit easier to find than the 8-inch. Of course, you can make tortillas without cake cutters. You can also use pot lids in appropriate sizes as long as the lids have sharp, well-defined edges. Just press the lid into the dough and wiggle back and forth a bit to create a sharp round edge all the way around.

Candy/deep-fry thermometer. You can't deep-fry properly without a simple candy/deep-fry thermometer to tell you that the oil has reached the proper temperature before you begin frying. An analog thermometer is sufficient. Take your pick of those on offer at amazon.com or your local kitchen supply store. There is very little daylight between them.

Digital food scale. For building any flour blend (page 4), you must have a simple digital scale, as measuring by volume, instead of by weight, is just too prone to error. For years, I had a digital scale made by Escali called the Primo that cost about twenty-five dollars. It lasted for years, until I dropped it in a bowl of water (then, inexplicably, it stopped working). I now have a super snazzy OXO scale that cost about ten dollars more than the Escali, and the display pulls out from the main portion of the scale so you can read it even if the bowl you have on the scale is large. To use a digital kitchen scale, simply turn it on, and then place a container on top of the scale and press "tare" to zero out the weight of the container. Select grams (kilograms) or ounces (pounds), place an ingredient in the bowl until the counter reaches the proper weight, then press "tare" again, and add the next ingredient. Continue as needed. A digital scale is also useful when using eggs in baking, as they are called for in various recipes. Eggs come in various sizes, and there are even some people lucky enough to have their own farm-fresh eggs available to them (in my dreams, I have backyard hens, but only in my dreams). The recipes in this cookbook call for large eggs, which typically weigh about 50 grams when weighed out of the shell. Rather than call out "large eggs" by name, however, I indicate the gram weight to accommodate our backyard farmers whose eggs are not of "standard" size.

Miniature deep fryer. If you are hesitant to deep-fry, or even if you find yourself avoiding a recipe simply because you don't want to handle a large quantity of oil, consider purchasing a miniature countertop deep fryer. I have a compact deep fryer made by Cuisinart, and I paid about forty dollars for it. It only holds about 1 liter of oil, and it makes frying quicker and easier by maintaining a consistent temperature automatically. It also forces you to deep-fry in small batches, which is always a good idea (see discussion, page 5).

Miniature muffin tins. Muffin tins are not something I would consider "special kitchen equipment," but miniature muffin tins are a different story—especially if you're making "small bites" recipes. Let's face it, small food is sometimes just too adorable to resist. That being said, miniature muffin tins seem to vary quite significantly in size and shape from brand to brand. After kissing a lot of miniature muffin tin frogs, I've found my prince. USA Pans 24-cup miniature muffin tins are my hands-down favorite. The wells are not too deep and not too shallow, and the shape is only slightly angled from the base to the top. In other words, they're *perfect*. (If you don't have miniature muffin tins, you can always use a standard 12-cup muffin tin, make half the amount, and bake for a few minutes longer.)

Mixer. You do not need a stand mixer for any of the recipes in this book, although it comes in handy. However, to make some of the doughs in Chapter 8, like the pretzel dough and pizza dough, you will need at least a five-speed handheld electric mixer with dough hooks. (You really do need a dough hook.)

Nut milk bag. A fine-mesh nylon bag, made for straining homemade nut milk, is very useful for squeezing liquid from vegetables such as spinach and zucchini. It is also useful for making nut milks.

Proofing bucket. Yeast bread dough that undergoes its first rise in the refrigerator must be sealed tightly in a container with a tight-fitting lid. Otherwise, the dough will dry out and not rise. I like to use plastic 2-quart Cambro brand food storage buckets, which seal tightly and are short enough to fit neatly on even the shortest refrigerator shelves.

Tortilla press. A metal tortilla press is ideal for making corn tortillas (page 202). I have one made by Vasconia, and it simply lasts and lasts. The simple masa dough is soft enough to be pressed into almost an ideal thickness with one motion of the press, and then I quickly roll it a bit thinner between two sheets of thick plastic or unbleached parchment paper, cut it with a cake cutter, and into the skillet it goes. I have not found it to be as useful when making any form of flour tortilla (page 198), but it is still somewhat helpful as a shortcut to get things started.

Unbleached parchment paper. For lining baking sheets, any parchment paper will do. For rolling out dough, I much prefer unbleached parchment paper, which is thinner and much more flexible. I buy If You Care brand unbleached parchment paper.

shoestring savings

It remains a fact of life that gluten-free ingredients, as well as gluten-free foods, are going to be more expensive for consumers than their conventional counterparts. The quintessential example is the all-purpose gluten-free flour blends discussed on pages 2 through 5. Since the ingredients in all-purpose gluten-free flours and gluten-free packaged goods are more expensive for manufacturers, it stands to reason that they are going to be more expensive for consumers. However, the additional markup that goes into prepared gluten-free foods can be avoided when you make your own at home.

Making the recipe at home can mean saving more than 70 percent of the cost. For example, shrimp pot stickers (page 141) cost less than 20 cents each to make. To buy them will set you back a full dollar each—and that's only if you get free shipping. Plus, you still have to cook them! Frozen gluten-free pierogi cost 60 cents each to buy and again only about 20 cents each to make. Prepared, frozen gluten-free egg rolls cost a whopping two dollars each; using the recipe on page 35 will cost 70 cents each. Pigs in blankets will cost 75 cents each when bought ready-made. To make them yourself costs 30 cents each. Keep in mind that most of these frozen gluten-free foods are not available in brick-and-mortar stores in most areas, even if you live in a major metropolitan area like I do. So you'll have to order them online, which most likely means you'll be buying them in bulk. What if you only want a few pigs in as many blankets?

Wraps and doughs, if you can find them anywhere to purchase, simply pale in comparison to homemade in taste, texture, and price. One large homemade gluten-free tortilla (page 198) will cost about 15 cents each to make and $1.11 to buy. Were you hoping for a wrap that you can actually bend and roll, one that doesn't crack? We both know you're going to have to make your own. Pizza dough (page 214) costs about 20 cents per ounce to make, and 80 cents per ounce if you buy it. And just imagine the difference in taste, texture, and quality.

In the interest of full disclosure, I will admit that purchasing certain prepared foods makes sense. I regularly purchase ready-made gluten-free corn tortillas, as they are widely available and inexpensive, and I find them useful in a pinch. But, of course, the superior texture and taste of a homemade corn tortilla would be questioned only by someone who has never had the pleasure.

chapter 2: deliciously fried

onion rings

IT'S AMAZING HOW TENDER AND SWEET A SLICE OF onion can become after it's soaked in buttermilk, then battered and fried to perfection. Soaking the onions in buttermilk serves a few important purposes: it tenderizes the texture of the onions, mellows any bite they might have, and helps the batter to adhere to the rings during frying. Although this recipe calls for soaking the onions for between 30 minutes and 1 hour, if they're fresh and crisp when you slice them, soaking in buttermilk for longer than an hour should be just fine. Once fully prepared, they are best eaten right away.

MAKES ABOUT 40 RINGS

2 large yellow or Vidalia onions, peeled and
   cut into ½-inch-thick rings
2 cups (16 fluid ounces) buttermilk, at
   room temperature
6 tablespoons (54 g) cornstarch, plus about
   1 cup more for dredging
¾ cup (120 g) superfine white rice flour
¼ teaspoon kosher salt
1 egg yolk, at room temperature
1 cup (8 fluid ounces) warm water
Neutral oil, for frying

NO-FRY OPTION: Although tempura batter is traditionally only used for frying, it's actually appropriate for baking as well. Your results won't be exactly the same, of course, but it's nice to have the alternative. Preheat your oven to 400°F, line a large baking sheet with aluminum foil, and grease it well with cooking oil spray. Prepare and batter the onions as directed in the recipe as written, but then place the onions on the prepared baking sheet about 1 inch apart from one another. Bake for about 20 minutes, or until lightly golden brown. Allow to cool for about 5 minutes before removing from the baking sheet and serving. This will allow the tempura to set so it doesn't stick to the baking sheet.

Place the onion slices in a large zip-top bag, cover with the buttermilk, and seal the bag. Allow to sit in the refrigerator for at least 30 minutes and up to 1 hour.

Prepare the tempura batter. In a large bowl, place the 6 tablespoons cornstarch, the white rice flour, and the salt, and whisk to combine well. In a small bowl, beat the egg yolk with the warm water until well combined. Create a well in the center of the large bowl with the cornstarch and white rice mixture, and pour in the water and egg yolk mixture in a slow and steady stream, whisking to combine constantly. The tempura batter should be about the consistency of heavy cream. Place about 1 cup of extra cornstarch in a shallow bowl for dredging, and set it aside with the tempura batter.

Place about 3 inches of frying oil in a medium-size, heavy-bottomed stockpot and bring to 360°F. Line a large rimmed baking sheet with paper towels, place a wire rack on top, and set it aside.

Remove the onions from the refrigerator and pull out the rings from the buttermilk one at a time, allowing the excess buttermilk to drip off. Dredge the onion rings though the extra cornstarch, then dip in the tempura batter and allow much of the tempura batter to drip off. Place the rings in the hot oil in small batches, taking care not to crowd the oil. The onion rings should begin to bubble up immediately. Fry until the bubbling subsides and the onion rings are lightly golden brown all over, about 2 minutes per side. Remove from the oil with a spider or slotted spoon, and place on the wire rack to drain completely. Return the oil to temperature before frying the remaining onion rings in small batches. Keep the early batches of onion rings warm in a 200°F oven, still on the racks above the paper towels.

jalapeño poppers

IF YOU'VE EVER TRIED TO FRY JALAPEÑO POPPERS yourself, you know that the real trick is getting the breadcrumb coating to "stick" to the peppers during frying. After you've gone through the whole dry-wet-dry breading process, you don't want to watch the breading slip right off into the frying oil, along with all your jalapeño popper hopes and dreams. Simply double-bread the peppers and allow them to "dry" a bit at room temperature after each coating. You'll be rewarded with the rich, creamy, spicy, and crunchy poppers that appetizer dreams are made of. Oh, and when handling the jalapeño peppers, be sure to wear disposable kitchen gloves (or you'll be sooooooorrrrryyyy).

Line a large rimmed baking sheet with parchment paper, place a wire rack on top, and set it aside.

Put on your plastic gloves, and cut a slit lengthwise in each pepper from the top to the bottom. Cut a slit across the very bottom of the pepper and another at the very top, creating an I shape, to expose the ribs and seeds. Pry the pepper open just enough to reach inside with the tip of a paring knife. Remove the ribs and seeds and set the peppers aside. In a medium-size bowl, place the cream cheese and Cheddar cheese and stir to combine well. Fill each pepper carefully with the cream cheese mixture, press the seam of the pepper closed, and squeeze gently to close.

In a small bowl, place the flour, salt, pepper, paprika, chili powder, and garlic powder, and whisk to combine well. Place the beaten eggs in a separate shallow bowl, and the breadcrumbs in a third. Dip the stuffed jalapeños into the flour mixture, then the beaten eggs, allowing the excess to drip off. Place each pepper into the breadcrumbs, pressing gently to help the breadcrumbs adhere on all sides, then on the baking rack. Allow the peppers to sit for about 10 minutes. Then, dip the peppers in the eggs and breadcrumbs again, then allow them to sit for 10 more minutes.

Place paper towels on a plate, and set it aside. Heat 2 inches of frying oil to 325°F in a medium-size, heavy-bottomed pan. Fry the stuffed peppers in batches until golden brown on all sides, making sure not to crowd the oil, about 5 minutes per batch. Remove the peppers from the oil with a strainer, and place on the paper-towel-lined plate to drain. Bring the oil back up to temperature before frying the remaining peppers. Serve warm.

MAKES 15 POPPERS

15 jalapeño peppers
1 8-ounce package cream cheese, at room temperature
6 ounces Cheddar cheese, shredded
½ cup (70 g) all-purpose gluten-free flour (page 2)
¼ teaspoon kosher salt
⅛ teaspoon freshly ground black pepper
⅛ teaspoon smoked paprika
⅛ teaspoon chili powder
¼ teaspoon garlic powder
3 eggs (150 g, weighed out of shell), at room temperature, beaten
1½ cups (180 g) panko-style gluten-free breadcrumbs, plus more as necessary
Neutral oil, for frying

———————— ⚹ ————————

MAKE-AHEAD OPTION: There are so few ingredients in the filling that it's not particularly useful to make it ahead of time. It is useful to prepare the jalapeños ahead of time by removing the seeds and ribs, and then storing them in a zip-top plastic bag in the refrigerator for up to 3 days. Once fried, these are best eaten right away.

NO-FRY OPTION: To bake the jalapeño poppers instead of frying them, preheat your oven to 375°F and line a large rimmed baking sheet with unbleached parchment paper. Slice the peppers in half horizontally to remove the seeds and ribs, fill each half with the filling, then coat the outside of each pepper in the dry ingredients, egg wash, and then the breadcrumbs. Place 1 inch apart from one another on the prepared baking sheet and bake until the filling is bubbling and the peppers are fork-tender, about 18 minutes. Allow to cool briefly before serving.

———————— ⚘ ————————

fried pickle chips

MAKES 48 CHIPS

1 (16-ounce) jar hamburger dill pickle chips
1½ cups (12 fluid ounces) buttermilk
2 cups (280 g) Basic Gum-Free Gluten-
    Free Flour (page 4)
1 teaspoon kosher salt
1 teaspoon smoked paprika
1 teaspoon ground cumin
⅛ teaspoon chili powder
Neutral oil, for frying

MAKE-AHEAD OPTION: The dry ingredients can be mixed together ahead of time and stored in a sealed container at room temperature for weeks. The pickles can be drained of their brine and soaked in buttermilk for up to an hour before breading and frying. Once fully prepared, they are best eaten right away.

NO-FRY OPTION: To make baked pickle chips, you'll need to add about 1 cup (120 g) of panko-style gluten-free bread-crumbs to the flour mixture for that crunch that you just won't get otherwise. Follow the directions as they are written, but instead of frying, preheat your oven to 400°F, line a rimmed baking sheet with unbleached parchment paper, grease the paper, and place the prepared pickle chips about 1 inch apart from one another. Bake for about 15 minutes, or until lightly golden brown all over.

FRIED PICKLE CHIPS ARE NOT AS FAMILIAR A SMALL bite as Stuffed Mushrooms (page 70) and Cheese Puffs (page 28), but the combination of briny pickles, smoky paprika and cumin, and just a touch of heat from chili powder, fried to golden perfection, will quickly become a new favorite. Fried pickle chips are delicious served with ranch dressing for dipping (page 103), or instead of fries with a nice, juicy hamburger.

Remove the pickle chips from the brining oil and place in a colander lined with paper towels to drain. Place the drained pickles in a medium-size bowl and cover with the buttermilk. Line a large rimmed baking sheet with parchment paper and place a wire rack on top. Set aside.

In a separate, medium-size bowl, place the flour, salt, paprika, cumin, and chili powder, and whisk to combine well. Remove the pickles from the buttermilk in batches, allowing the excess to drip off, then dredge them through the flour mixture. Shake off any excess flour and place them on the wire rack. Allow them to sit for 10 minutes.

Heat about 2 inches of oil in a medium-size, heavy-bottomed pot to 325°F. Place the pickles in batches in the hot oil and fry until golden brown all over, about 4 minutes per batch. Remove the pickles from the oil with a spider or slotted spoon and place back on the wire rack to drain. Bring the oil back to temperature in between batches until all of the pickles are fried.

mozzarella sticks

MAKES 20 STICKS

1 egg (50 g, weighed out of shell), at room
temperature

¾ cup (6 ounces) milk, at room temperature, plus more as necessary

1 cup (140 g) Basic Gum-Free Gluten-Free
Flour (page 4)

1 teaspoon ground cumin

½ teaspoon chili powder

½ teaspoon kosher salt

1 ounce Parmigiano-Reggiano cheese,
finely ground

20 mozzarella sticks

1½ cups (180 g) panko-style gluten-free
breadcrumbs, plus more as necessary

Neutral oil, for frying

Tomato sauce, for serving

NO-FRY OPTION: Although they simply
won't be the same, these mozzarella sticks
can be baked instead of fried. Simply
follow the recipe instructions for coating
the cheese in the egg and flour mixture,
then the breadcrumbs, but instead of
frying, place them about 1 inch apart from
one another on a large baking sheet lined
with unbleached parchment paper. Bake in
a 375°F oven for about 15 minutes, or until
lightly golden brown all over. Serve warm.

*IF YOU'VE EVER BEEN TO A DINER, THEN YOU HAVE A
working familiarity with fried mozzarella sticks. Sticks of cheese
are coated in a lightly spiced egg and flour mixture, then coated
in breadcrumbs and fried until crisp and golden. Since mozzarella cheese is, hands down, the cheese with the most delightful
"pull," it's an ideal candidate for deep-frying—and eating hot!
Try making it a complete meal by slicing the mozzarella sticks
into 4 chunks each, then proceeding with the recipe as written.
Serve the warm fried mozzarella bites over a big salad. Once
completely prepared, they are best eaten right away.*

In a small bowl, place the egg and milk, and whisk to combine
well. Set the mixture aside. In a separate large bowl, whisk the
flour, cumin, chili powder, salt, and Parmigiano-Reggiano cheese
until well combined. Create a well in the center of the dry ingredients, add the egg yolk and milk mixture, and whisk until very
well combined. The batter should be thickly pourable. If it is too
thick, whisk in more milk by the teaspoonful until it reaches the
proper consistency.

Line a large serving platter with paper towels and set aside.
In a deep fryer or medium-size, heavy-bottomed pot, place
about 2 inches of oil, and bring the oil to 350°F over medium-
high heat. Dip the cheese sticks into the batter, allowing any
excess batter to drip off, then roll in the breadcrumbs to coat
completely. Place the breaded cheese sticks in the hot oil with
tongs, a few at a time, taking care not to crowd the oil. Stir occasionally to ensure that the cheese sticks don't stick to the frying
pan and that they fry evenly. Fry until golden brown all over,
about 4 minutes total per batch.

Using a spider strainer, remove the fried cheese sticks from
the hot oil and place on the paper-towel-lined platter to drain.
Bring the oil back to temperature between batches. Serve
immediately with marinara sauce for dipping.

arancini

ARANCINI *IS TYPICALLY MADE WITH LEFTOVER*
risotto. But I find that creamy cooked risotto is just not quite
sticky enough for shaping into balls that can hold together
during frying. I prefer to make arancini *with cooked sushi rice,*
which is super starchy. Just be sure that all of your ingredients
for making the rice balls are at room temperature before you
combine them, or the mixture will not hold together well. All of
the shaping should be done with very wet hands, as that will help
keep the rice from sticking to your hands. Wet them often. Your
reward is fried rice balls that somehow manage to be crispy and
creamy all at the same time. Serve with plenty of tomato sauce
for dipping!

MAKES 8 BALLS

1½ cups (210 g) cooked sushi rice (arborio rice can be used if necessary), at room temperature

½ teaspoon kosher salt

¼ teaspoon freshly ground black pepper

1 teaspoon dried oregano

1 ounce finely grated Parmigiano-Reggiano cheese, at room temperature

1 egg (50 g, weighed out of shell), at room temperature, beaten

1½ ounces low-moisture mozzarella cheese, roughly chopped (into about ½-inch-square cubes)

About ½ cup (70 g) Basic Gum-Free Gluten-Free Flour, plus more as necessary (page 4)

Egg wash (1 egg beaten with 1 tablespoon milk), for dipping

1½ cups (180 g) panko-style gluten-free breadcrumbs, plus more as necessary

Neutral oil, for frying

Tomato sauce, for serving

Line a rimmed baking sheet with unbleached parchment paper and set it aside. In a large bowl, place the cooked rice, salt, and pepper and mix to combine. Place the dried oregano in the palm of one hand and rub it with the forefinger of the other to release the herb's oils before adding it to the rice mixture. Add the Parmigiano-Reggiano cheese and the beaten egg, and mix to combine well. With wet hands, divide the mixture into 8 portions of equal size. Place the chopped mozzarella nearby. Divide each portion of the rice mixture in half: set aside half and press the other half firmly into one wet palm. With your free hand, place 2 small cubes of mozzarella cheese in the center of the rice in your palm. Place the remaining half of the rice mixture on top of the cheese cubes, and (again with very wet hands) squeeze the mixture closed as tightly as you can, then roll into a ball. Set the filled rice ball on the prepared baking sheet. Repeat with the remaining 7 parts of the rice mixture. Place the baking sheet in the refrigerator to chill until firm, about 15 minutes.

Place the Basic Gum-Free Gluten-Free Flour blend in a shallow bowl, the egg wash in another shallow bowl, and the breadcrumbs in a final shallow bowl. Remove the rice balls from the refrigerator or freezer. Dredge each rice ball through the flour blend, then through the egg wash (allowing any excess to drip off), and finally in the breadcrumbs until well coated on all sides. Return to the baking sheet. Place the coated rice balls in the refrigerator while you heat the oil.

Place paper towels on a plate, and set it aside. In a medium-size, heavy-bottomed pot or fryer, place about 3 inches of frying oil over medium-high heat. Bring the oil to 375°F. Remove the rice balls from the refrigerator, and fry in small batches until cooked through and golden brown all over, about 6 minutes total. Bring the oil back to temperature between batches. Transfer the rice balls to the paper-towel-lined plate and serve warm, with tomato sauce.

MAKE-AHEAD OPTION: These can be shaped and filled ahead of time, but not breaded, and then frozen in a single layer on a baking sheet. Pile the frozen rice balls into a freezer-safe bag and place in the freezer until ready to use. Defrost at room temperature before breading and frying. Once fully prepared, they are best eaten right away.

NO-FRY OPTION: The rice balls can be stuffed and shaped, then breaded and baked instead of fried. Preheat your oven to 350°F and line a large rimmed baking sheet with unbleached parchment paper. Place the breaded rice balls on the baking sheet about 1 inch apart from one another, brush sparingly with an egg wash (1 egg beaten with 1 tablespoon water) and bake until lightly golden brown all over, about 20 minutes. Serve warm.

BIGGER BITE OPTION: Double the recipe and make the portions twice as large. Frying time will need to be increased by about another 3 minutes total.

zucchini fritters

MAKES 10 FRITTERS

2 pounds fresh zucchini, trimmed and
shredded
1 pound Yukon Gold potatoes, peeled and
shredded
1 medium shallot, peeled and shredded
3 eggs (150 g, weighed out of shell), at
room temperature, beaten
2 teaspoons baking powder
1½ teaspoons kosher salt
¾ cup (105 g) Basic Gum-Free Gluten-
Free Flour (page 4)
Vegetable oil, for shallow frying

MAKE-AHEAD OPTION: The raw fritters
are too soft and fragile to be made ahead
of time, but the shredded zucchini and
potatoes can be wrung out and stored in a
sealed container in the refrigerator for up
to 3 days. Allow the zucchini and potatoes
to sit at room temperature for about 10
minutes before using in the recipe. Once
fully prepared, they are best eaten right
away.

NO-FRY OPTION: The fritters can be baked
instead of shallow fried. Preheat your oven
to 375°F and line a large rimmed baking
sheet with unbleached parchment paper.
Place the shaped patties on the baking
sheet about 1 inch apart from one another.
Place in the center of the preheated
oven and bake for about 18 minutes, or
until lightly golden brown all over. Serve
immediately.

WHEN IT'S SUMMERTIME AND ZUCCHINI IS EVERY-
where, zucchini fritters (along with zucchini cake, zucchini bread,
and zucchini muffins) are a must. They use up a fair amount of zuc-
chini, always a summertime virtue, and, especially when paired
with shredded potatoes and shallots, taste and smell like heaven.
The starch in the potatoes helps the fritters hold together well
once they're cooked and helps keep the amount of flour neces-
sary to a minimum.

Place the shredded zucchini in the center of a clean tea towel
or a nut milk bag. Gather the edges of the towel or nut milk bag
tightly around the zucchini and squeeze as hard as you can to
eliminate as much liquid from the zucchini as possible. Transfer
the zucchini to a large bowl. Repeat with the shredded potatoes, and place them in the bowl with the zucchini.

In a separate small bowl, place the shallot, eggs, baking powder, salt, and flour, and whisk to combine well, working out any
lumps in the flour. Add the egg and flour mixture to the bowl of
shredded zucchini and potatoes, and mix to combine well.

Place paper towels on a plate, and set it aside. Heat about
¼ inch of vegetable oil in a cast-iron or stainless-steel skillet
over medium heat until the oil shimmers. With wet hands, shape
some of the raw zucchini mixture into a baseball-size ball and
gently squeeze out as much moisture as possible. Shape into
a patty about 3½ inches in diameter, and place in the frying
pan. Repeat with as many more patties as you can fit in the pan
without overlapping them. Fry the patties for 3 minutes; flip and
fry for another 3 minutes or until the patties seem firm to the
touch. Remove to the paper-towel-lined plate, and repeat with
the remaining batter. Serve immediately.

fried green tomatoes

LATE IN THE SUMMER SEASON, I START REALLY ROOT-ing for all of the tomatoes in my garden to finish the year strong. Go tomatoes go! Inevitably, some of them will stay green despite my best intentions. Since large beefsteak tomatoes are the most likely candidates to stay green, it's lucky that fried green tomatoes call for unripe beefsteaks. Breathe new life into those stragglers by dredging them in flour, a milk-and-egg wash, and then a crispy crunchy mix of cornmeal and panko-style breadcrumbs. Shallow-fry them to tender, crispy perfection. Long live the green tomato! Once fully prepared, they are best eaten right away.

Lay out the tomato slices on a flat surface, sprinkle them evenly with the salt and pepper, and set aside briefly. Create dipping stations with three shallow bowls. In one shallow bowl, place the gum-free flour, in another beat together the milk and eggs, and in a third, whisk together the cornmeal and breadcrumbs.

Place paper towels on a plate, and set it aside. In a large cast-iron or stainless-steel skillet over medium heat, heat about ¼ inch of oil until it shimmers. Dredge each tomato slice in the flour, then the egg mixture, and finally the breadcrumb mixture, pressing the tomato slice into the mixture on both sides to help it adhere to the tomatoes. Place as many of the prepared tomato slices in the hot skillet as will fit without overlapping, and cook for about 6 minutes, flipping halfway through, until lightly golden brown all over. Remove to the paper-towel-lined plate to drain. Serve immediately.

3 large green beefsteak tomatoes, cut into ½-inch-wide slices

1 teaspoon kosher salt

⅛ teaspoon freshly ground black pepper

1 cup (140 g) Basic Gum-Free Gluten-Free Flour (page 4)

½ cup (4 fluid ounces) milk

2 eggs (100 g, weighed out of shell)

5 tablespoons (40 g) coarsely ground yellow cornmeal

1 cup (120 g) panko-style gluten-free breadcrumbs, plus more as necessary

Neutral oil, for shallow frying

NO-FRY OPTION: To bake green tomatoes until tender but crispy, preheat your oven to 400°F, line a rimmed baking sheet with unbleached parchment paper, and place the prepared green tomato slices about 1 inch apart from one another on the baking sheet. Bake for about 18 minutes, or until lightly golden brown all over and fork-tender.

cheddar hush puppies

LEGEND HAS IT THAT HUSH PUPPIES ARE SO NAMED because these delicious little fried corn cakes were tossed to yapping dogs to keep them quiet during the American Civil War. Me, I'll give dog food to the dogs and keep these golden brown on the outside, soft and tender on the inside nuggets for myself and my guests. My favorite way to serve these corn cakes is on a bed of greens dressed with a simple vinaigrette and a dollop of sour cream. Once fully prepared, they are best eaten right away.

In a large bowl, place the flour, cornmeal, baking powder, baking soda, and salt, and whisk to combine well. Add the grated cheese, scallions, and celery, and mix to coat them in the dry ingredients. Create a well in the center and add the buttermilk and eggs. Mix until just combined, without overmixing. The batter should be thick but soft.

Place paper towels on a plate, and set it aside. Bring 2 inches of oil to 325°F in a large, heavy-bottomed pot or deep fryer. Using a spring-loaded ice cream scoop or two large spoons, drop about 2 tablespoons' worth of batter in the hot oil. Repeat with as much batter as can fit comfortably, taking care not to crowd the oil. Allow to cook for about 3 minutes or until golden brown on one side before gently turning over and cooking until golden brown all over and cooked through, about another 2 minutes. Remove from the oil with a strainer and place on the paper-towel-lined plate to drain. Bring the oil back to temperature between batches. Repeat with the remaining batter. Serve immediately.

MAKES 12 LARGE HUSH PUPPIES

- 1 cup (140 g) all-purpose gluten-free flour (page 2)
- 1 cup (132 g) coarsely ground yellow cornmeal
- 1 teaspoon baking powder
- 1/2 teaspoon baking soda
- 3/4 teaspoon kosher salt
- 3 ounces sharp yellow Cheddar cheese, grated
- 1/4 cup chopped scallions (about 2 large scallions)
- 2 tablespoons minced celery (from 1 small stalk)
- 1 cup (8 fluid ounces) buttermilk, at room temperature
- 2 eggs (100 g, weighed out of shell), at room temperature, beaten
- Neutral oil, for deep-frying

BIGGER BITE OPTION: Drop the cornmeal batter in the frying oil in larger portions, about 1/4-cup each, and fry for 4 to 5 minutes more.

NO-FRY OPTION: The only way to achieve a round shape for your hush puppies is to fry them, but that alone isn't reason enough not to bake them if that's what you'd prefer. Prepare and portion the batter in the same manner as directed in the recipe, but preheat your oven to 350°F and place the batter portions spaced about 11/2 inches apart from one another on a lined rimmed baking sheet. Bake the hush puppies for about 15 minutes, or until lightly golden brown all over. Serve immediately.

---

cheese puffs

IF YOU'RE LOOKING FOR MINIMUM EFFORT AND MAX-imum impact, then cheese puffs are the way to go. The recipe is a riff on a classic French choux pastry, which gets its airy "puff" from the relatively high proportion of eggs in the dough. If you've never made that sort of pastry dough before, you might be tempted to think of it as fussy and hard to master. But when you read through the recipe, you'll see just how easy it really is. Particularly since they're so small, these little bites hold their shape perfectly after baking, and their golden-brown color makes for quite an impressive presentation.

MAKES ABOUT 30 PUFFS

1 cup (8 fluid ounces) milk

4 tablespoons (56 g) unsalted butter, chopped

¾ teaspoon (5 g) kosher salt

1 cup (140 g) Gluten-Free Pastry Flour (page 5)

4 eggs (200 g, weighed out of shell), at room temperature, beaten

4 ounces sharp yellow Cheddar cheese, grated

———————⚓———————

MAKE-AHEAD OPTION: Make the pastry dough ahead of time; place it in a sealed container and store in the refrigerator for up to 5 days. Allow the dough to come to room temperature before piping and baking as directed. Cheese puffs are best eaten the same day they are baked.

BIGGER BITE OPTION: Pipe about 12 mounds of pastry dough, each about 2 inches in diameter. Bake at 375°F for 20 minutes. Working quickly, remove the baking sheet from the oven and slice a small slit on the side of each pastry. Return to the oven and continue to bake for 5 minutes or until pale golden all over. Turn off the oven and open the oven door slightly. Allow the puffs to sit in the oven until the temperature falls to about 200°F on your oven thermometer, about 15 minutes. Remove from the oven and serve.

———————⚓———————

Preheat your oven to 375°F. Line a rimmed baking sheet with unbleached parchment paper and set it aside.

In a medium-size saucepan, place the milk, butter, and salt and cook over medium heat until the butter is melted and the mixture begins to simmer. Remove the pan from the heat, and add the pastry flour, stirring vigorously. Return the pan to the heat, and continue to stir vigorously until the mixture pulls away from the pan and comes together in a ball, about 2 minutes. Set the mixture aside to cool until no longer hot to the touch, about 3 minutes.

Transfer half the dough to a blender or food processor. Pour the beaten eggs on top and then add the rest of the dough. Pulse the blender or food processor until the mixture is smooth and uniformly well blended. Add the cheese, and pulse until it is uniformly distributed throughout the dough.

Transfer the dough from the blender or food processor to a pastry bag fitted with a large plain piping tip about 1 inch in diameter. Pipe the dough into 30 small rounds, each about ¾ inch in diameter, onto the prepared baking sheet, about 2 inches apart from one another. With wet fingers, gently smooth the tops of the pastries so that nothing will burn during baking. Bake the cheese puffs in the center of the preheated oven until pale golden, about 15 minutes. Serve warm.

fried wontons

ALTHOUGH WONTONS ARE TYPICALLY BOILED OR steamed, frying them brings its own sort of crispy, crunchy pleasure. These fried wontons are filled with a mouthwatering mix of ground meat, fresh ginger, garlic, scallion, soy sauce, and oyster sauce, along with chopped kale. Chopped spinach can be substituted for the kale, but it must be cooked (if fresh) or defrosted (if frozen), and then drained of all liquid, since water is the enemy of frying. If you plan to bake the wontons, or boil them in soup, a wetter vegetable like bok choy is delicious and no cause for concern.

Make the wonton wrappers according to the recipe instructions.

In a large bowl, add the meat, ginger, garlic, scallion, soy sauce, oyster sauce, and kale and mix well to combine.

To assemble the wontons, place a wonton wrapper flat in the palm of your hand. Add 1 teaspoon of mixture to the center of the wrapper. Using a finger or pastry brush, paint the edges of the wonton wrapper with the egg wash. Fold one corner of the wrapper catty-corner to the opposite corner to enclose the filling. Seal tightly all around, squeezing out any air.

Place paper towels on a plate, and set it aside. Place about 1½ inches of oil in a medium-size, heavy-bottomed saucepan, and bring the oil to 350°F over medium-high heat. Add a few wontons to the oil to fry, turning occasionally until they are golden brown, about 3 minutes. Remove them using a strainer to the paper-towel-lined plate to drain. Bring the oil back to temperature between batches. Repeat with the remaining wontons. Serve warm, with extra soy sauce for dipping or sweet chili sauce.

MAKES ABOUT 50 WONTONS

1 recipe Wonton Wrappers (page 191)
1 pound ground pork or beef
1 tablespoon finely grated fresh ginger (or 1½ teaspoons ground ginger)
2 garlic cloves, peeled and finely minced
1 scallion, finely chopped
1 tablespoon gluten-free soy sauce or tamari, plus more for dipping
2 tablespoons gluten-free oyster sauce
2 cups finely chopped kale
Egg wash (1 egg beaten with 1 tablespoon water)
Neutral oil, for frying

———————— ⚜ ————————

MAKE-AHEAD OPTION: The wontons can be shaped and filled, then placed in a single layer on a baking sheet and frozen. Pile them into a freezer-safe bag and return them to the freezer. Defrost overnight in the refrigerator and pat dry before frying. Fried wontons are best eaten right away for maximum crispness.

NO-FRY OPTION: Follow the recipe instructions as written for shaping and filling the wontons, but line a large rimmed baking sheet with unbleached parchment paper and set it aside. Place the raw shaped and filled wontons on the prepared baking sheet about 1 inch apart from one another. Using a pastry brush, coat the tops with an egg wash (1 egg beaten with 1 tablespoon water), then place in the center of the preheated oven and bake for about 12 minutes or until lightly golden brown. They can also be boiled in hot soup until tender and cooked all the way through, about 5 minutes.

BIGGER BITE OPTION: Prepare them instead like Egg Rolls (page 35).

———————— ⚘ ————————

crab rangoon

MAKES 36 WONTONS

1 8-ounce package cream cheese, at room
temperature

1 8-ounce container crème fraîche, at room
temperature

2 tablespoons (15 g) confectioners' sugar
(optional)

2 tablespoons tamari or gluten-free soy
sauce

1 tablespoon gluten-free Worcestershire
sauce

2 garlic cloves, peeled and minced

8 ounces lump crabmeat

Neutral oil, for frying

MAKE-AHEAD OPTION: I do not recommend filling and shaping these ahead. The filling ingredients, without the crabmeat, can be made up to 2 days in advance and stored in a sealed container in the refrigerator. When you're ready to serve the Rangoon, just fold the crabmeat into the filling, shape the dumplings, and finish the recipe. Once fried, crab Rangoon are best eaten right away.

NO-FRY OPTION: Place the shaped crab Rangoon puffs on an oven-safe wire rack positioned above a rimmed baking sheet. Spray generously with nonstick cooking spray, and bake at 375°F until lightly golden brown all over, about 18 minutes. Serve warm.

HAVE YOU EVER BEEN TOLD THAT THE CHINESE FOOD that we eat in the United States is nothing like the food that the Chinese eat in China? Well, if that's true, then crab Rangoon must be Exhibit One in making that argument successfully. If that was meant to scare me off from enjoying these little savory pockets of creamy crabmeat, it didn't work at all. They're "traditionally" made with a touch of confectioners' sugar in the filling, which is how the recipe is written here, but personally I prefer them without it, as it lets the gentle sweetness of the cream cheese shine. Be sure to buy lump crabmeat, which has large chunks of that beautiful meat. I buy it prepackaged in the refrigerated section of my local grocery store.

Prepare the wonton wrappers. In the bowl of a stand mixer with the paddle attachment or a large bowl with a hand mixer, beat the cream cheese, crème fraîche, and sugar until smooth. Add the tamari, Worcestershire sauce, and garlic, and beat again until well combined. Using a spatula, carefully fold in the crabmeat, being careful not to mince it.

Place paper towels on a plate, and set it aside. In a heavy-bottomed saucepan or deep fryer, heat about 3 inches of oil to 350°F. Line a large rimmed baking sheet with unbleached parchment paper and set it aside. Line up 6 to 8 wonton wrappers on a separate parchment-lined work surface. Set up a small bowl with lukewarm water alongside the wrappers. Dip your fingers in the water bowl, and use them to wet the entire border of each of the wrappers. Place about 1 teaspoon of filling in the center of each wonton wrapper. Gather together all of the sides of the wrappers toward the center, carefully eliminating all trapped air as you work. Press together all the edges with wet fingers. Place on the prepared baking sheet about 1 inch apart from one another. Repeat with the remaining wrappers and filling. Blot the filled wontons dry with a paper towel.

Place the filled wontons in the hot oil in batches, taking care not to crowd the oil. Fry for about 2 minutes per side, or until golden brown all over. With a slotted spoon or spider, remove Rangoon puffs to the paper-towel-lined plate to drain. Bring the oil back to temperature between batches. Repeat with the remaining wonton wrappers and serve warm.

egg rolls

THE SECRETS TO MAKING PERFECT FRIED EGG ROLLS that easily crackle and shatter in your mouth the moment you bite into them are twofold. First, you must roll your wonton wrappers (page 191) thin enough to be truly translucent. The wonton wrapper dough is rather easy to work with, and the best way to roll it paper thin is to roll the dough a bit thicker, cut it into smaller squares than you'll need for the recipe, and then roll each individual square again. Second, your oil must be hot enough before frying to keep the egg rolls from absorbing the oil. Oil at the proper temperature will quickly cook the outside of the roll and seal it from coming into contact with any more oil.

Make the wonton wrappers according to the recipe instructions, cover them with a moist paper towel, and set them aside.

In a large bowl, place the tamari, rice vinegar, honey, and 2 tablespoons of the flour, and whisk to combine well. Pour half the sauce into a separate, small bowl. To the remaining sauce in the large bowl, add the ground meat and mix gently to combine. Allow to sit at room temperature for a few minutes to allow the beef to absorb the sauce.

In a large skillet, cook the garlic in the sesame oil over medium heat until fragrant, about 2 minutes. Remove the garlic from the oil and discard it. Add the cabbage and carrots to the oil, add the remaining sauce, and toss to combine. Turn the heat down to medium low; cover the skillet and cook, tossing occasionally, until the cabbage is wilted and the carrots are beginning to soften, about 5 minutes. Uncover the skillet, add the beef mixture and the remaining tablespoon flour, and toss to combine. Allow the mixture to cool for about 10 minutes. Tilt the skillet to separate any remaining liquid; pour off and discard the liquid.

Arrange the first wonton wrapper square with a corner facing you. Place about 2 tablespoons of the filling about 1 inch from the corner of the wrapper. Fold over the corner and roll one turn away from yourself, making sure to roll as tightly as possible and to prevent any trapped air bubbles. Fold in the sides securely, and continue to roll until the egg roll is completely sealed. Repeat with the remaining wrappers and filling.

MAKES 15 EGG ROLLS

1 recipe Wonton Wrappers (page 191), rolled very thin and cut into 6-inch squares

6 tablespoons tamari or gluten-free soy sauce

2 tablespoons rice vinegar

2 tablespoons (42 g) honey

3 tablespoons (27 g) Basic Gum-Free Gluten-Free Flour (page 4), divided

1 pound 90% lean ground beef

4 garlic cloves, smashed and peeled

2 tablespoons sesame oil

10 ounces shredded cabbage

2 large carrots, peeled and grated

Neutral oil, for frying

Line a large rimmed baking sheet with unbleached parchment paper, place a wire rack on top, and set it aside. Place about 1 inch of oil in a medium-size, heavy-bottomed saucepan, and bring the oil to 350°F over medium-high heat. Fry the egg rolls in batches until golden brown all over, about 2 minutes per side, taking care not to crowd the oil. Remove to the wire rack to drain. Return the oil to temperature between batches. Serve warm.

—————— ✤ ——————

MAKE-AHEAD OPTION: The filling can be made up to 3 days ahead of time and stored in a sealed container in the refrigerator. The wonton wrappers can also be dusted with flour, stacked, wrapped tightly, and refrigerated for 3 days and frozen for up to 2 months, and then defrosted in the refrigerator before using. The egg rolls themselves can also be assembled completely, then wrapped tightly and refrigerated for 3 days or frozen for up to 2 months, and then defrosted in the refrigerator. Just be sure to pat the outside of the egg rolls dry before frying. Once fried, egg rolls are best eaten right away but can be wrapped and stored in the refrigerator for a day or two before eating cold.

NO-FRY OPTION: These egg rolls can be placed on a lined baking sheet about 1 inch apart from one another, brushed generously with neutral cooking oil, and baked at 375°F for about 20 minutes or until lightly golden brown all over.

—————— ♧ ——————

falafel

ALTHOUGH YOU CAN USE CANNED CHICKPEAS TO make falafel (with fine results), traditional falafel is made with dried chickpeas that have been soaked overnight in room temperature water and then drained, but not cooked before they are processed and fried. The soaked chickpeas are not quite tender and not quite crunchy, and after being processed and then cooked, they are never ever mushy. Soaking dried beans overnight requires almost no effort at all, very little advance planning, and is the only way to enjoy the garlicky wonder that is real falafel. If serving falafel as an appetizer, offer a dipping sauce made of 1 cup of plain yogurt mixed with 1 tablespoon of freshly squeezed lemon juice. Otherwise, serve in a hummus-smeared wrap.

Place the chickpeas in a large bowl, add enough tap water to cover them by about 2 inches, and soak overnight or for at least 8 hours. Drain the soaking water from the chickpeas.

In the bowl of a food processor fitted with a steel blade, place the chickpeas, onion, parsley, cilantro, garlic, flour, baking powder, salt, pepper, and cumin. Process on high speed until a thick paste forms, about 5 minutes. Add more flour by the teaspoonful as necessary to hold the mixture together when it is squeezed. Turn the falafel mixture out into a large bowl, cover, and refrigerate for at least 30 minutes or until chilled.

Place paper towels on a plate, and set it aside. Using wet hands, shape the mixture into balls about the size of golf balls, rolling tightly. Place about 2 inches of oil in large, heavy-bottomed pot, and bring the oil to about 360°F over medium-high heat. Place the falafel balls in the hot oil in batches, taking care not to crowd the oil, and allow to fry for 3 to 4 minutes, rotating once during frying, until golden brown all over. Transfer to the paper-towel-lined plate to drain. Bring the oil back to temperature between batches. Repeat with the remaining dough and serve warm.

MAKES ABOUT 15 BALLS

8 ounces dried garbanzo beans (chickpeas)
1 small yellow onion, peeled and roughly chopped
3 tablespoons chopped fresh parsley
3 tablespoons chopped fresh cilantro
2 garlic cloves, peeled
¼ cup (35 g) Basic Gum-Free Gluten-Free Flour (page 4), plus more as necessary
1 teaspoon baking powder
1 teaspoon kosher salt
¼ teaspoon freshly ground black pepper
1 tablespoon ground cumin
Neutral oil, for frying

MAKE-AHEAD OPTION: The falafel can be shaped ahead of time, frozen in a single layer on a baking sheet, then piled into a freezer-safe container and returned to the freezer until ready to use. Defrost overnight in the refrigerator. If frying, allow to sit at room temperature until no longer wet to the touch before placing in the hot oil.

NO-FRY OPTION: To bake instead of fry your falafel, preheat your oven to 400°F. Line a large rimmed baking sheet with unbleached parchment paper, then place shaped falafel 1 inch apart from one another. Brush the balls generously with extra-virgin olive oil, then place in the center of the preheated oven to bake until lightly golden brown on top and brown on the underside, about 15 minutes. Serve warm.

BIGGER BITE OPTION: These can be shaped into about 8 patties instead of 15 balls, then baked or fried as directed. You will need to watch the baking or frying time, but it doesn't change much as the patties are larger, but not nearly as thick as the balls.

samosas

THESE LIGHTLY SPICED, SAVORY DUMPLINGS ARE TRA-ditionally deep-fried, but they are also delicious when baked (see "No-Fry Option" below). However you prepare them, they're at their best when served with plenty of sweet red chili sauce (Thai Kitchen brand is gluten-free in the United States). They're the perfect appetizer and are even lovely for a light dinner when served with a nice big salad.

MAKES 25 SAMOSAS

1 recipe Empanada Dough (page 189)
2 large russet potatoes, peeled and diced
3 tablespoons (42 g) extra-virgin olive oil
1 small yellow onion, peeled and diced
1 garlic clove, peeled and minced
½ teaspoon freshly grated ginger (or ¼ teaspoon dried ginger)
2 ounces chopped canned green chiles
1 tablespoon finely chopped fresh cilantro
1½ tablespoons freshly squeezed lemon juice
½ teaspoon turmeric
½ teaspoon garam masala
½ teaspoon chili powder
¼ teaspoon kosher salt
Egg wash (1 egg beaten with 1 tablespoon water)
Neutral oil, for frying

—————————— ⚜ ——————————

MAKE-AHEAD OPTION: The filling can be made up to 3 days ahead of time and stored in a sealed container in the refrigerator. The empanada dough can also be dusted with flour, stacked, wrapped tightly, and refrigerated for 3 days and frozen for up to 2 months and then defrosted in the refrigerator before using. The samosas themselves can also be assembled completely, frozen in a single layer on a baking sheet, then placed in a freezer-safe bag, wrapped, frozen for up to 2 months, and then defrosted in the refrigerator. Just be sure to pat the outside of the samosas dry before frying. Once fried, they are best eaten right away.

NO-FRY OPTION: Place the shaped samosas on an oven-safe wire rack positioned above a rimmed baking sheet. Spray generously with nonstick cooking spray, and bake at 375°F until lightly golden brown all over, about 18 minutes. Serve warm.

—————————— ⚜ ——————————

Prepare the empanada dough according to the recipe instructions, cutting out 4-inch squares, gathering and rerolling scraps. Sprinkle the empanada squares lightly with extra flour, then stack them and place them in the refrigerator to chill while you prepare the filling.

Bring a large pot of water to a boil over medium-high heat and add the diced potatoes. Return the water to a boil and boil the potatoes until fork-tender, about 5 minutes. Drain the water, pat the potatoes dry, and set them aside to cool.

In a large saucepan over medium heat, place the oil and heat until rippling. Add the onion and sauté over medium heat, stirring occasionally, for 5 minutes. Add the garlic, and cook until the garlic is fragrant and the onion is translucent, about another 2 minutes. Add the potatoes to the pan and cook, stirring frequently, until they have begun to brown, about 5 minutes. Remove the saucepan from the heat and add the ginger, chiles, cilantro, lemon juice, turmeric, garam masala, chili powder, and salt and mix to combine. Set the filling aside to cool.

Place the squares of empanada dough on a flat surface and brush off any excess flour. Place about 1½ tablespoons of filling on one half of each square of dough, leaving ¼ inch bare. Paint the edges of the dough lightly with the egg wash, and fold the dough up and over the filling, matching one corner to the opposite one, pressing out any air. Press the edges to seal.

Place paper towels on a plate, and set it aside. Place about 2 inches of frying oil in a large, heavy-bottomed saucepan, and bring the oil to 350°F over medium-high heat. Place the shaped samosas in the frying oil in batches, taking care not to crowd the oil, and fry until golden brown all over, about 3 minutes on each side. Remove from the oil using a spider or a slotted spoon and place on the paper-towel-lined plate to drain. Bring the oil back to temperature between batches. Serve warm.

potato croquettes

POTATO CROQUETTES ARE MY IDEA OF GROWN-UP tater tots—but with a beautifully crisp outside and a light and creamy center. I insist upon adding scallions and parsley to the mixture since it brightens the flavor without making the croquettes taste spicy. The best way to make perfect mashed potatoes is with a food mill, but a ricer does the job as well—as does a fork if that's all you have. Resist the urge to mash them in a food processor or blender. The potatoes will lose their texture and become gummy, making the croquettes impossible to shape without heaps of extra flour, which will destroy their flavor.

First, make the mashed potatoes. Place the potatoes, with the skins still on, in a large pot and cover with cold, salted water by about 2 inches. Cover the pot, bring to a boil over medium heat, and allow to cook for about 30 minutes, or until the potatoes are fork-tender. Remove from the heat and drain the water. While the potatoes are still warm, remove the skins and pass the potatoes through a ricer or a food mill or mash completely with a fork. Add the butter and milk, and mix until well combined and smooth.

Line two large baking sheets with waxed paper and set them aside. In a large bowl, place the mashed potatoes and stir to loosen them a bit. Add the salt, pepper, scallions, parsley, and eggs and mix to combine. Add ½ cup flour, and stir until just absorbed. Using an ice-cream scoop, scoop 3 dozen portions of the mixture and place about 1 inch apart from one another on the prepared baking sheet. Place the baking sheet in the refrigerator to chill for at least 15 minutes or until firm.

Set up a dipping station with three shallow bowls: one with about 1 cup of flour, one with the egg wash, and one with the breadcrumbs. Dip each chilled croquette in the flour, tossing gently to coat all sides, then in the egg wash on all sides (shaking off any excess), and finally in the breadcrumbs on all sides, pressing gently to adhere. Return to the baking sheet and allow to sit for 10 minutes.

Place paper towels on a plate, and set it aside. Bring about 2 inches of oil in a large, heavy-bottomed saucepan to about 325°F. Fry the croquettes in small batches, taking care not to crowd the pan, until golden brown all over, about 3 minutes per side. Remove from the oil using a spider or a slotted spoon and place on the plate to drain. Bring the oil back to temperature between batches. Serve warm.

MAKES 36 CROQUETTES

2 pounds Yukon Gold potatoes
4 tablespoons (54 g) unsalted butter, at room temperature
¾ cup (6 fluid ounces) milk, at room temperature
½ teaspoon kosher salt
¼ teaspoon freshly ground black pepper
2 tablespoons chopped scallions (white and green parts)
3 tablespoons chopped fresh flat-leaf parsley (or 1½ tablespoons dried)
2 eggs (100 g, weighed out of shell), beaten
½ cup (70 g) all-purpose gluten-free flour (page 2), plus more for dredging, divided
Egg wash (2 eggs beaten with 1 tablespoon milk)
1 cup (120 g) panko-style gluten-free breadcrumbs, plus more as necessary
Neutral oil, for frying

MAKE-AHEAD OPTION: The mashed potatoes, using the first three ingredients, can be made up to 3 days ahead of time and stored in the refrigerator. Once fried, they are best eaten right away.

NO-FRY OPTION: If you would prefer to bake these croquettes instead of frying them, make them approximately half as large as directed in the recipe, then place about 1 inch apart from one another on a lined baking sheet and bake at 375°F until lightly golden brown all over and crisp, about 20 minutes. Serve warm.

coconut shrimp

MAKES 24 SHRIMP

1 cup (60 g) unsweetened coconut chips, plus more as necessary

¾ cup (90 g) panko-style gluten-free breadcrumbs, plus more as necessary

½ cup (70 g) Basic Gum-Free Gluten-Free Flour (page 4), plus more as necessary

½ teaspoon kosher salt

¼ teaspoon freshly ground black pepper

Egg wash (2 eggs beaten with 1 tablespoon milk)

1 pound raw large easy peel shrimp, peeled and deveined, tails still attached

Neutral oil, for frying

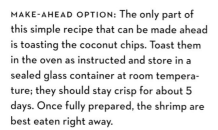

MAKE-AHEAD OPTION: The only part of this simple recipe that can be made ahead is toasting the coconut chips. Toast them in the oven as instructed and store in a sealed glass container at room temperature; they should stay crisp for about 5 days. Once fully prepared, the shrimp are best eaten right away.

NO-FRY OPTION: To bake instead of frying these, preheat your oven to 375°F. Place the prepared raw shrimp on a wire rack positioned above a rimmed baking sheet lined with unbleached parchment paper. Spray the tops of the shrimp with cooking oil spray, and bake for about 15 minutes or until crisp and lightly golden brown. Serve warm.

FROZEN SHRIMP TEND TO BE LESS EXPENSIVE THAN fresh—and, unless you are buying them nearly right off the boat, frozen ones are just as fresh as those you'll find at the fish counter. If you're comfortable removing the "vein" on your own, then you don't need to buy them deveined. You can only go wrong when buying shrimp in one of two ways: by buying shrimp from the fish counter that actually smells fishy (which means it's old), or by buying already cooked shrimp, which is impossible to heat at all without overcooking. Easy peel shrimp are always deveined, and the shell comes off easily, in one large piece. This recipe is a great way to make shrimp that pleases nearly everyone, and it really lets the shrimp shine. I like to serve these slightly sweet, almost crunchy shrimp over thin Asian rice noodles with some blanched sugar snap peas for a simple meal, and of course they're perfect as appetizers.

Preheat your oven to 300°F. Line a large rimmed baking sheet with unbleached parchment paper and place the coconut chips on it in a single, even layer. Place the baking sheet in the center of the preheated oven and bake for 5 minutes. Remove the baking sheet from the oven, and use a spoon to redistribute the chips. Bake until the chips are very lightly golden brown on the edges, about 5 more minutes, then set aside to cool.

Line a large rimmed baking sheet with waxed paper and set it aside.

Crush the cooled coconut chips into small pieces, place with the breadcrumbs in a medium-size shallow bowl, and stir to combine. Set up a dipping station of three shallow bowls: one with the ½ cup flour mixed with the salt and pepper, one with the egg wash, and one with the breadcrumb and coconut mixture. Dip each shrimp in the flour mixture on all sides, then in the egg wash on all sides (shaking off any excess), and finally in the breadcrumbs and coconut on all sides, pressing gently to adhere. Place on the lined baking sheet and allow to sit for 10 minutes.

Place paper towels on a plate, and set it aside. Place about ½ inch of oil in a large, heavy-bottomed saucepan and heat until rippling. Fry the shrimp in small batches, taking care not to crowd the pan, until lightly golden brown all over, about 3 minutes on each side. Remove from the oil using tongs and place on the paper-towel-lined plate to drain. Serve warm.

chapter 3: hearty meat-based snacks

pigs in blankets

PIGS IN BLANKETS ARE, QUITE SIMPLY, THE VERY FIRST appetizer to disappear at a party. These little smoky bites wrapped in dough and baked until golden are hard to resist. I prefer to pair the yeasty taste of pizza dough with the weenies, rather than the buttery taste of pastry. But if you'd prefer, you can use the recipe for Basic Pastry and Biscuit Dough (page 186) in its place. Simply follow the directions as written, except first shape and wrap the pastry dough around the weenies and then chill until the dough is firm before baking.

Make the pizza dough according to the recipe instructions and place in a sealed container or bowl in a warm, draft-free location to rise until nearly doubled in size (1 to 2 hours, depending upon environment). Full doubling is not necessary. Place the risen dough, still in a sealed container or bowl, in the refrigerator to chill until firmer, about 30 minutes.

Preheat your oven to 400°F. Line a rimmed baking sheet with unbleached parchment paper and set it aside. Divide the chilled dough into 6 pieces of roughly equal size, and with floured hands shape each piece into a ball. Place one ball of dough at a time (covering the others with a moist towel), on a well-floured surface, dust lightly with extra flour, and roll into a rectangle 8 inches long by 6 inches wide and ¼ inch thick, dusting with flour if the dough becomes sticky. With a sharp knife or pastry wheel, slice into 4 smaller rectangles, each 2 inches wide by 6 inches long. Repeat with the remaining 5 balls of pizza dough.

Assemble the pigs in their blankets. With a sharp knife, slash each weenie on one side, along its length about halfway through to allow steam to escape. Position a prepared rectangle of dough with a short side facing you, place a weenie on the edge of the short side and roll it tightly away from you. Place the pig and blanket on the prepared baking sheet, seam-side down. Repeat with the remaining rectangles and weenies, and place them about 1 inch apart from one another on the baking sheet. Brush the blankets lightly with the egg wash.

Place the baking sheet in the center of the preheated oven and bake until the dough is brown around the edges and lightly brown on top, about 12 minutes. Remove from the oven, and allow to cool briefly before serving.

1 recipe Thin Crust Pizza Dough
(page 214)
8 ounces gluten-free cocktail weenies, blotted dry*
Egg wash (1 egg beaten with 1 tablespoon warm water)

Be sure to blot the hot dogs dry quite well. Otherwise, the pizza dough will slip right off the dogs after they're wrapped.

———————— ⚓ ————————

MAKE-AHEAD OPTION: The pizza dough can be made up to 5 days ahead of time and stored in a well-sealed proofing bucket or other secure container in the refrigerator. Shaping the dough and wrapping the weenies should be done right before baking, and they are then best eaten right away once baked.

BIGGER BITE OPTION: In place of cocktail weenies, use full-size hot dogs. Shape the pizza dough into rectangles that are 6 inches by 4 inches, and roll in similar fashion. Increase the baking time to about 20 minutes or until brown around the edges and lightly brown on top.

———————— ⚓ ————————

miniature corn dogs

WHETHER YOU CONSIDER THEM STREET FOOD, FOOD truck food, or county fair food, there's nothing quite like the feeling of biting into a corn dog. The cornbread coating is delightfully crisp on the outside and soft and fluffy inside and pairs perfectly with the smokiness of the hot dog. If you are dead set against using hot dogs but you have a favorite vegetarian or nonbeef substitute, I bet that would work just fine.

MAKES 16 CORN DOGS

½ cup (66 g) coarsely ground yellow cornmeal

½ cup (70 g) Basic Gum-Free Gluten-Free Flour (page 4)

1 tablespoon (12 g) sugar

2 teaspoons baking powder

½ teaspoon kosher salt

1 egg (50 g, weighed out of shell), at room temperature, beaten

½ cup (4 fluid ounces) milk, at room temperature

8 gluten-free hot dogs, each cut by cross-section into two equal pieces

16 bamboo skewers or lollipop sticks

Neutral oil, for frying

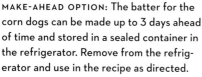

MAKE-AHEAD OPTION: The batter for the corn dogs can be made up to 3 days ahead of time and stored in a sealed container in the refrigerator. Remove from the refrigerator and use in the recipe as directed. Once fully prepared, they are best eaten right away.

NO-FRY OPTION: I'm going to be honest. The no-fry option for corn dogs is less than ideal, as the cornmeal batter tends to spread out on the baking sheet, making for a thin underside. That being said, if you'd like to bake these instead of frying them, there is no need to boil the hot dogs first. Preheat your oven to 375°F and line rimmed baking sheets with unbleached parchment paper. Follow the recipe instructions for preparing the dogs, but instead of frying them, place them on the baking sheet about 2 inches apart from one another and bake until lightly golden brown all over, about 15 minutes.

In a small bowl, place the cornmeal, flour, sugar, baking powder, and salt, and whisk to combine well. Add the egg and milk, and mix to combine well. Place the mixture in an 8-inch-tall glass, and place the glass in the refrigerator.

Boil the hot dogs. Place 5 cups of water in a medium-size saucepan and bring to a boil. Place the hot dogs in the boiling water, cover, and remove the saucepan from the heat. Allow to sit for 7 minutes. Remove the hot dogs from the water and dry them thoroughly with paper towels. You will need 16 bamboo skewers or lollipop sticks. Place a skewer or lollipop stick in the cut end of each hot dog and push through so that the stick is about halfway into the hot dog, and set the hot dogs aside.

Place the frying oil in a medium-size, heavy-bottomed saucepan, and bring the oil to 350°F over medium-high heat. Remove the cornmeal mixture from the refrigerator, and mix to loosen it. Slowly immerse the hot dogs on the sticks, one at a time, in the glass, removing slowly to allow the cornmeal coating to adhere to the hot dog. Holding the sticks, immerse the coated hot dogs in the frying oil and fry for about 3 minutes or until the coating is uniformly deep golden brown. Remove the hot dog from the frying oil, and place on a paper towel to cool briefly. Bring the oil back to temperature between batches. Repeat with the remaining hot dog halves. Serve immediately.

pretzel dogs

THERE'S NOTHING QUITE LIKE THE CRISPY OUTSIDE of a soft pretzel that gives way to the fluffy soft interior, and when hidden inside is a perfectly cooked hot dog, you know you've got a winner. I'm partial to dipping pretzel dogs in spicy mustard, but if you're all about ketchup, I promise not to judge. As with the other hot dog recipe, if you have a favorite vegetarian hot dog, it can be substituted in this recipe. To miniaturize these pretzel dogs, in place of hot dogs, try using miniature cocktail weenies as in Pigs in Blankets (page 47). Once baked, these are best enjoyed right away.

Prepare the pretzel dough according to the recipe instructions. Line two rimmed baking sheets with unbleached parchment paper and sprinkle generously with flour or spray with cooking oil. Set the baking sheets aside.

Turn the dough out onto a piece of lightly floured parchment paper, divide it into two portions, and cover one with a moist tea towel. Dust the top of the other portion of dough generously with flour, and roll it into a 20 x 10-inch rectangle, dusting with flour as necessary to keep the dough from sticking. Cut the rectangle along the width into 8 strips, each 1¼ inches wide. Sprinkle the strips of dough with flour. Wrap each strip tightly around a hot dog in a spiral, overlapping the dough on itself a bit more closely toward the center, beginning and ending ½ inch from each of the ends of the hot dog. Press the edges of the dough gently but firmly to seal. Place the hot dogs a couple of inches apart on a prepared baking sheet, seam side down. Cover with plastic wrap and place in a warm, draft-free environment; allow to rise until just about doubled in volume (around 45 minutes). Repeat with the rest of the dough and the remaining 8 hot dogs, all the dough rising at the same time.

Preheat your oven to 375°F and place the baking soda bath in a large heavy-bottomed pot on the stovetop to boil over high heat. Once the dough is done rising, place the rolls a few at a time into the boiling baking soda bath for less than a minute. Remove the rolls with a strainer and return to the baking sheet. Brush the tops with the egg wash. Sprinkle with coarse salt to taste. Place the baking sheet in the center of the preheated oven and bake until golden brown all over, about 20 minutes. Allow to cool briefly on the pan before serving.

MAKES 16 DOGS

1 recipe Gluten-Free Pretzel Dough (page 213)

16 gluten-free all-beef hot dogs, blotted dry*

Baking soda bath for boiling (6 cups water plus 1 tablespoon baking soda plus 1 teaspoon salt)

Egg wash (1 egg beaten with 1 tablespoon milk)

Kosher coarse salt, to taste

Be sure to blot the hot dogs dry quite well. Otherwise, the pretzel dough will slip right off the dogs after it is coiled around them.

sticky barbecue chicken wings

3 pounds chicken wings

1 cup (8 fluid ounces) tomato ketchup

¼ cup (55 g) packed light-brown sugar

2 tablespoons white wine vinegar

1 tablespoon gluten-free Worcestershire sauce

2 teaspoons smoked Spanish paprika

1 teaspoon onion powder

1 tablespoon freshly squeezed lemon juice

DELICIOUSLY STICKY BARBECUE CHICKEN WINGS ARE incredibly easy to make, and only take about 30 minutes to bake in the oven. So why include slow cooker directions? Because when you're making wings, you're undoubtedly making something else. No one is going to make a whole meal of just wings, no matter how savory and delicious they are. After a quick spin under your oven's broiler, if you make these wings in the slow cooker, your oven stays free and your kitchen stays cool. When the wings are nearly done in the slow cooker, try popping the Miniature Mac and Cheese Cups (page 91) in the oven and serving them together—along with a cold beer. Pub food at home! These wings are best eaten right away once cooked.

Oven directions. Preheat your oven to 425°F. If you prefer, cut the tips off the chicken wings and discard them, then separate the wings into a drum and a flat. Place all of the wings in a large casserole dish. Place all of the remaining ingredients in the order listed in a large bowl, and whisk to combine well. Pour the sauce over the top of the wings and toss them to coat completely. Place in the center of the preheated oven and cook for 25 to 30 minutes, or until the wings are cooked through and the sauce has begun to caramelize.

Slow cooker directions. Grease or line a large rimmed baking sheet with parchment paper and set it aside. If you prefer, cut the tips off the chicken wings and discard them, then separate the wings into a drum and a flat. Place the wing pieces on the baking sheet in a single layer and drizzle lightly with 2 tablespoons of extra-virgin olive oil, ¼ teaspoon kosher salt, and ⅛ teaspoon freshly ground black pepper. Place under your oven's broiler about 4 inches from the flame and heat for 10 minutes, turning once, until the wings have just begun to brown.

Grease the liner of a 6-quart slow cooker. Place all of the remaining ingredients in the order listed in a large bowl, and whisk to combine well. Transfer the hot wings to the greased slow cooker liner, cover with the sauce, and toss to coat. Cook in the slow cooker for 4 to 5 hours on low, or 2½ hours on high, until the wings are cooked all the way through.

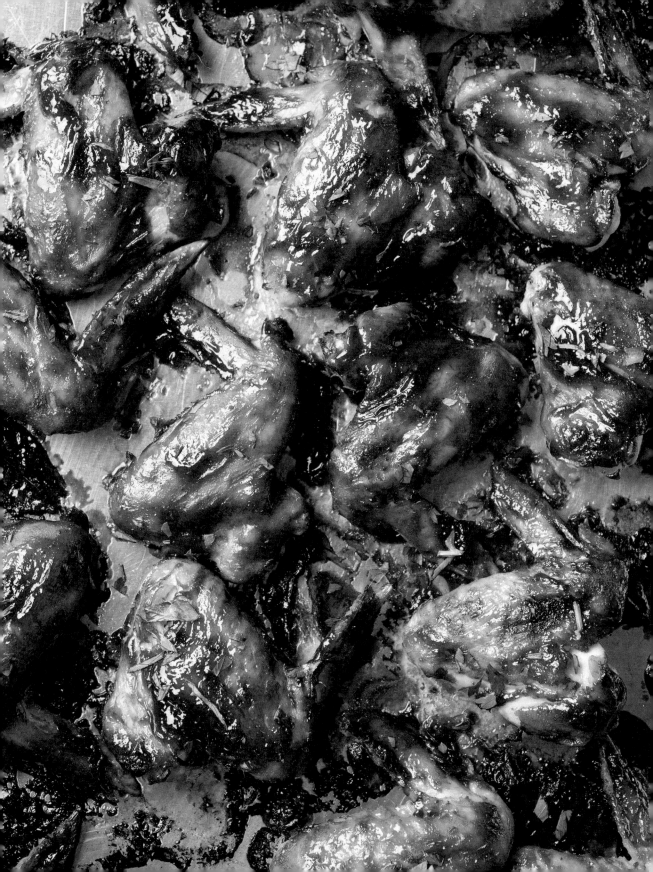

buffalo chicken meatballs

THESE SAVORY CHICKEN MEATBALLS MADE WITH shallots, carrots, and celery are already packed with tons of flavor even before we add the hot-as-you-want-it-to-be buffalo sauce. Luckily, Frank's Hot Sauce is gluten-free and widely available, and my favorite just happens to be the buffalo-style variety. But if you have another favorite hot sauce, or you like a superhot variety of Frank's, don't let me stand in your way. I don't consider myself a total spicy-food wimp, but I'm not out to prove anything either. Served over white rice with a dinner salad, these make a delightful main dish.

Preheat your oven to 400°F. Grease a 13 x 9-inch pan and set it aside.

In a large bowl, place all of the meatball ingredients except for the ground chicken in the order listed and beat to combine well. Add the ground chicken, and mix gently to combine. The ground chicken will be soft and can be overworked rather easily. Pull off golf-ball-size pieces of the meatball mixture and shape gently into rounds between wet palms. You should be able to form about 24 meatballs. Place them about 1 inch apart from one another in the prepared pan. Place the pan in the oven and bake for about 20 minutes or until the meatballs are cooked through completely.

While the meatballs are baking, make the buffalo sauce. In a medium, heavy-bottomed saucepan, melt the butter over medium heat. Once the butter has melted, add the garlic cloves and sauté until fragrant, about 2 minutes per side. Remove and discard the garlic, add the hot sauce, vinegar, and Worcestershire sauce, and whisk until well combined. Remove the sauce from the heat.

Once the meatballs have finished baking, remove them from the oven and pour the buffalo sauce over the top. Toss the meatballs to coat them in the sauce, and serve on a platter with the optional blue cheese dressing and extra hot sauce.

MAKES 24 MEATBALLS

FOR THE MEATBALLS

2 medium stalks celery, minced
2 large carrots, shredded
1 small shallot, peeled and minced
1 egg (50 g, weighed out of shell), beaten
1 cup (120 g) panko-style gluten-free breadcrumbs
½ teaspoon kosher salt
¼ teaspoon freshly ground black pepper
1½ pounds white meat ground chicken

FOR THE BUFFALO SAUCE

4 tablespoons (56 g) unsalted butter
2 garlic cloves, smashed and peeled
2 to 4 tablespoons gluten-free hot sauce, to taste, plus extra for serving
1 tablespoon white wine vinegar
⅛ teaspoon gluten-free Worcestershire sauce (I like Lea & Perrins)
Blue cheese dressing, for serving (optional)

———————— ⚓ ————————

MAKE-AHEAD OPTION: The meatballs can be shaped ahead of time and frozen raw in a single layer on a baking sheet, then wrapped tightly in freezer-safe wrap and returned to the freezer. Defrost in the refrigerator overnight, then bake and continue with the recipe as instructed. The sauce should be made right before serving. Once fully prepared, the meatballs without the sauce can also be cooled, wrapped tightly, and frozen. Defrost in the refrigerator before gently reheating with the sauce in a saucepan over low heat.

BIGGER BITE OPTION: Make the meatballs twice as big! Just keep an eye on baking time, which will increase to about 35 minutes.

———————— ⚓ ————————

swedish meatballs

IT'S HARD TO IMAGINE A TRADITIONAL BUFFET WITH-out a chafing dish full of lightly spiced, deeply flavorful pork-and-beef Swedish meatballs. The sauce is really a gravy with the light umami taste of soy sauce and vinegar. You can omit the cream and still have a delicious sauce, but I really like the smoothness that just that touch of cream adds. Serve them as an appetizer, or over a plate of wide, flat gluten-free noodles for a hearty and satisfying meal.

MAKES ABOUT 36 MEATBALLS

FOR THE MEATBALLS

3 egg yolks (75 g), at room temperature, beaten

½ cup (4 fluid ounces) milk, at room temperature

1 cup (120 g) panko-style gluten-free breadcrumbs

1 small onion, peeled and minced

¼ teaspoon ground allspice

1 teaspoon kosher salt

¼ teaspoon ground black pepper

1 pound ground pork

1 pound 90% lean ground beef

FOR THE SAUCE

2 tablespoons (28 g) unsalted butter

3 tablespoons (27 g) Basic Gum-Free Gluten-Free Flour (page 4)

1 tablespoon gluten-free soy sauce

½ teaspoon apple cider vinegar

¼ teaspoon freshly ground black pepper

3 cups (24 fluid ounces) chicken stock

3 tablespoons heavy whipping cream

Fresh flat-leaf parley, chopped

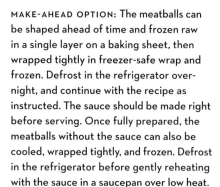

MAKE-AHEAD OPTION: The meatballs can be shaped ahead of time and frozen raw in a single layer on a baking sheet, then wrapped tightly in freezer-safe wrap and frozen. Defrost in the refrigerator over-night, and continue with the recipe as instructed. The sauce should be made right before serving. Once fully prepared, the meatballs without the sauce can also be cooled, wrapped tightly, and frozen. Defrost in the refrigerator before gently reheating with the sauce in a saucepan over low heat.

BIGGER BITE OPTION: Make them twice as big! Just keep an eye on baking time, which will increase to about 35 minutes.

First, make the meatballs. Preheat your oven to 350°F. Line a rimmed baking sheet with unbleached parchment paper, and set it aside.

In a medium-size bowl, place the egg yolks and milk and whisk together. Add the breadcrumbs, minced onion, allspice, salt, and pepper, and mix to combine well. Add the pork and beef, and mix until well combined. Using wet hands, shape the mixture into golf-ball-size balls and place on the prepared baking sheet about 1 inch apart from one another. Place in the center of the preheated oven and bake for about 20 minutes or until firm to the touch and cooked through.

Make the sauce. In a large sauté pan over medium-high heat, melt the butter. Add the flour and cook, whisking constantly, until it has begun to brown slightly and smells nutty, about 1 minute. Add the soy sauce, vinegar, and pepper, whisking to combine after each addition. Add the chicken stock slowly, whisking constantly; bring to a simmer and cook until the sauce has begun to thicken, about 6 minutes. Finish by adding the cream, whisking constantly, and return to a simmer. Add the cooked meatballs to the sauce and simmer, turning occasion-ally to coat with the sauce, until heated through. Serve with chopped parsley.

cheesy, smoky sausage balls

WHAT HOLIDAY WOULD BE COMPLETE WITHOUT SAUsage balls? Smoked paprika mixes and mingles with the sweetness of the onion and the anise in the sweet Italian sausage, and it just smells like home. The dry ingredients are essentially the makings of a pancake mix, which is probably why the leftovers taste so good for breakfast the next morning.

Preheat your oven to 350°F. Line a large rimmed baking sheet with unbleached parchment paper, and set it aside.

In a large bowl, place the flour, baking powder, baking soda, salt, pepper, and paprika, and whisk to combine well. Add the grated Cheddar cheese, and toss to coat the cheese in the dry ingredients. Add the grated onion, butter, and egg, and mix to combine well. Add the sausage and mix, then knead with your hands to bring the mixture together.

Divide the mixture into 24 pieces, about 2 tablespoons each. Roll each piece between your palms very tightly into balls, and place about 1 inch apart from one another on the prepared baking sheet. After forming all of the balls, roll each one a second time in your palms to ensure they are pressed together tightly or they will fall apart during baking. Replace balls on baking sheet.

Place in the center of the preheated oven and bake until golden brown and cooked through, about 25 minutes. Remove from the oven and allow to cool briefly before serving.

MAKES 24 SAUSAGE BALLS

1 cup (140 g) Basic Gum-Free Gluten-Free Flour (page 4)
1 teaspoon baking powder
¼ teaspoon baking soda
¾ teaspoon kosher salt
⅛ teaspoon freshly ground black pepper
¾ teaspoon smoked Spanish paprika
8 ounces sharp yellow Cheddar cheese, grated
1 small yellow onion, peeled and grated
4 tablespoons (56 g) unsalted butter, melted and cooled
1 egg (50 g, weighed out of shell), at room temperature, beaten
1 pound gluten-free sweet Italian sausage, casings removed

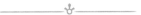

MAKE-AHEAD OPTION: Sausage balls can be shaped ahead of time and frozen raw in a single layer on a baking sheet, then wrapped tightly in freezer-safe wrap and returned to the freezer. Defrost in the refrigerator overnight, then continue with the recipe as instructed. Once baked, they can be cooled, wrapped tightly, and then refrigerated or frozen. If frozen, defrost in the refrigerator, then heat in a warm oven.

sweet and sour meatballs

FOR THE MEATBALLS

1 egg (50 g, weighed out of shell), beaten

1 medium onion, peeled and grated

1 cup (120 g) panko-style gluten-free breadcrumbs

½ teaspoon kosher salt

⅛ teaspoon freshly ground black pepper

1 teaspoon garlic powder

1½ pounds 90% lean ground beef

2 tablespoons (28 g) neutral cooking oil

FOR THE SAUCE

¾ cup (164 g) packed light-brown sugar

3 tablespoons (45 g) tomato ketchup

¼ cup apple cider vinegar

2 tablespoons tamari or gluten-free soy sauce

MAKE-AHEAD OPTION: The meatballs can be shaped ahead of time and frozen raw in a single layer on a baking sheet, then wrapped tightly in freezer-safe wrap and returned to the freezer. Defrost in the refrigerator overnight, then continue with the recipe as instructed. The sauce should be made right before serving. Once fully prepared, the meatballs without the sauce can also be cooled, wrapped tightly, and frozen. Defrost in the refrigerator before gently reheating with the sauce in a skillet over low heat.

BIGGER BITE OPTION: Make the meatballs twice as big! Just keep an eye on cooking time, which will increase to 40 to 45 minutes.

SWEET AND SOUR MEATBALLS HAVE A FEW INGREDI-ents in common with Buffalo Chicken Meatballs (page 55), but with none of the spice of hot sauce. These sweet and savory meatballs are cooked in a skillet along with the finger-licking-good sauce. They're the ideal party food when served on a skewer with a thick chunk of pineapple and are also delicious served over a nice sticky short-grain rice.

In a medium-size bowl, place the egg, onion, breadcrumbs, salt, pepper, and garlic powder, and beat to combine well. Add the ground beef, and mix gently but thoroughly with your hands. Shape the mixture into golf-ball-size balls.

In a large skillet over medium heat, heat the oil. Place the meatballs in a single layer in the oil, and cook, turning over, until browned on all sides.

In a large bowl, whisk together all of the sauce ingredients. Pour the sauce over the meatballs in the skillet, and bring the mixture to a boil. Reduce the heat to a simmer and cook, stirring frequently, until the meatballs are cooked all the way through and the sauce is thickened, about 30 minutes. Serve warm.

baked fish sticks

MY FAVORITE FIRM WHITE FISH TO BUY IS TILAPIA FOR one reason and one reason only: it tends to be the cheapest white fillet. And my kids love it. (I guess that's two reasons, but it wouldn't much matter how little it cost if my family wouldn't eat it.) It's hard for anyone to argue with a firm white fish so mild in taste and unobjectionable in texture, especially when it's coated in a basic breadcrumb mixture and baked. If you can't find tilapia, flounder or cod fillets also work well here. Whether baked or fried, they come out flaky and fresh tasting—and your house won't smell like fish afterward. As with any fish, once fully prepared, they are best eaten right away.

Preheat your oven to 375°F. Line a large rimmed baking sheet with unbleached parchment paper, set a large wire cooling rack on top, spray the wire rack generously with cooking oil spray, and set it aside. Set up a dipping station with three different shallow bowls. Place the flour, salt, and pepper in one, and whisk to combine. Place the eggs and milk in a second bowl, and beat until well combined. Place the breadcrumbs in the third.

Dredge all sides of the fish in the flour, shaking off excess, then dip in the egg wash, and allow any excess to drip off the fish. Finally, place the fish pieces in the breadcrumbs and press to coat the fish with the crumbs evenly on both sides. Place each piece of prepared fish on the wire rack. Spray the tops of all of the fish generously with cooking oil spray, and place in the preheated oven. Bake for 15 minutes or until very lightly golden brown and cooked through. Allow the fish sticks to cool briefly on the racks before serving, as they will stick to the rack if you try to remove them immediately.

MAKES ABOUT 24 FISH STICKS

¼ cup (35 g) Basic Gum-Free Gluten-Free Flour, plus more as necessary (page 4)
½ teaspoon kosher salt
⅛ teaspoon freshly ground black pepper
2 eggs (100 g, weighed out of shell)
2 tablespoons milk
2 cups (240 g) panko-style gluten-free breadcrumbs, plus more as necessary
1 pound firm white fish fillets (flounder, cod, or tilapia work well), sliced into strips 3 inches long by ¾ inch wide

FRY OPTION: Instead of baking these fish sticks, they can be fried. Place about 1 inch of neutral oil in a heavy-bottomed saucepan, and bring the oil to 350°F. Taking care not to crowd the oil, place the breaded fish sticks in the hot oil in batches and fry until lightly golden brown all over and cooked through (about 5 minutes total, turning halfway through frying). Remove from the oil using a spider or a slotted spoon and place on a paper-towel-lined plate to drain. Serve warm.

BIGGER BITE OPTION: Prepare the fish without slicing it into strips, and bake for about 25 minutes total, depending upon the size of the fillets.

chicken taquitos

IF YOU TAKE ONE LOOK AT THE CAN OF CHOPPED mild green chiles that this recipe calls for and roll your eyes at my wimpy palate, remember that I have young children. Besides, you can always substitute spicier canned green chiles for my mild ones. You can make these with store-bought corn tortillas, but freshly made corn tortillas make all the difference in these lightly spiced roll-ups. If you are looking to save time, try using shredded rotisserie chicken and you won't compromise on flavor.

Preheat your oven to 400°F. Place the chicken breasts about 1 inch apart from one another in a 12 x 9-inch baking dish. Drizzle the chicken breasts with 2 tablespoons of the olive oil, then sprinkle with ½ teaspoon salt and ⅛ teaspoon pepper. Spray the underside of a large piece of parchment paper, large enough to cover the whole baking dish, with cooking oil, and place, oiled-side down, directly on top of the chicken breasts in the pan. Place the pan in the oven and bake until the chicken reaches 165°F on an instant-read thermometer, about 30 minutes. Remove the chicken from the oven and shred with two forks while it's still warm. Place the shredded chicken in a medium-size bowl and set it aside. In a medium-size skillet, heat the remaining 2 tablespoons of olive oil and the butter over medium heat until the butter is melted and the oil is hot. Add the garlic, and cook until brown and fragrant, about 2 minutes. Discard the garlic, and add the chopped onion and the remaining salt and pepper. Cook the onions, stirring frequently, until they're translucent, about 6 minutes. Add the chopped chiles, and stir to combine. Add the mixture to the bowl of chicken, and mix to combine.

Line a large rimmed baking sheet with parchment paper, and set it aside. Open the first tortilla and brush one side with olive oil, and then invert it onto a flat surface. Scatter about 1 tablespoon of cheese on top of the tortilla in an even layer, leaving a ½-inch border clean. Top with about ⅛ of the chicken mixture in an even layer, again leaving a ½-inch border clean, and follow with another tablespoon of shredded cheese. Press down gently to help the filling adhere to the tortilla. Roll the tortilla tightly from one side to another, sealing in the filling. Place, seam-side down, on the prepared baking sheet. Repeat with the remaining tortillas and filling, placing the taquitos about ½ inch apart from one another. Brush the tops of the taquitos lightly with oil, then place the baking sheet in the oven and bake for 10 to 12 minutes or until lightly golden brown all over. Serve immediately, with lime.

MAKES 8 TAQUITOS

1 pound skinless, boneless chicken breasts
4 tablespoons (56 g) extra-virgin olive oil, divided, plus more for brushing
1 teaspoon kosher salt, divided
¼ teaspoon freshly ground black pepper, divided
1 tablespoon (14 g) unsalted butter
2 garlic cloves, smashed and peeled
1 medium-size onion, peeled and diced
1 4-ounce can chopped mild green chiles
8 6-inch gluten-free corn tortillas (use fresh [page 202] or store-bought), warmed in a hot, dry skillet until flexible
8 ounces Monterey Jack cheese, grated
1 lime, sliced, for serving

MAKE-AHEAD OPTION: The chicken can be made ahead of time and refrigerated or frozen in a sealed container. Defrost overnight in the refrigerator before using. The taquitos themselves can also be assembled completely, secured with toothpicks, then frozen in a single layer on a baking sheet before being transferred to a freezer-safe container and frozen. Defrost overnight in the refrigerator, then place in a baking dish, brush with oil, and bake as directed. Once baked, they are best eaten right away.

FOR THE CHICKEN

1 pound skinless, boneless chicken breasts, cut into 1-inch-square pieces

1½ cups (12 fluid ounces) buttermilk

1½ cups (210 g) Basic Gum-Free Gluten-Free Flour (page 4), plus more as necessary

2 teaspoons garlic powder

¼ teaspoon onion powder

2 teaspoons smoked paprika

1 teaspoon kosher salt

⅛ teaspoon freshly ground black pepper

Neutral oil, for frying

FOR THE WAFFLES

¾ cup (105 g) Basic Gum-Free Gluten-Free Flour

¼ teaspoon xanthan gum

3 tablespoons (27 g) cornstarch

1 teaspoon baking powder

¼ teaspoon baking soda

¼ teaspoon kosher salt

¼ teaspoon mustard powder

2 ounces sharp yellow Cheddar cheese, shredded

1½ teaspoons chopped chives

1½ tablespoons (21 g) neutral cooking oil

⅞ cup (7 fluid ounces) milk, at room temperature

1 egg (50 g, weighed out of shell), at room temperature, separated

CHICKEN AND WAFFLES SEEMS TO HAVE GAINED notoriety during the cultural renaissance in Harlem, New York, during the 1920s, '30s, and '40s, when restaurants stayed open late to accommodate jazz performers. Since it was essentially too late for dinner but too early for breakfast, a combination of fried chicken from the previous night's dinner service and early morning waffles started as a way to compromise—and increase sales. Then again, some in the American South also lay claim to the dish. Whatever its origins, the appeal of a combination of crispy waffles and tender fried chicken morsels is undeniable. Here, we just make them into party food by miniaturizing the pair.

Place the chicken in a large zip-top bag and pour in the buttermilk. Seal the bag tightly and place it in the refrigerator to soak for at least 30 minutes and up to overnight. Once the chicken has finished soaking, in a large bowl place the flour, garlic powder, onion powder, paprika, salt, and pepper, and whisk to combine. Remove the chicken from the refrigerator. Remove the pieces of chicken from the buttermilk one at a time, allowing excess buttermilk to drip off, and place them in the bowl with the flour mixture; discard the buttermilk. Once all of the chicken has been added to the bowl, toss the chicken to coat completely in the flour mixture. Allow the chicken to sit in the flour mixture while you make the waffles.

Preheat your waffle iron according to the manufacturer's directions. In a large bowl, place the flour, xanthan gum, cornstarch, baking powder, baking soda, salt, and mustard powder, and whisk to combine well. Add the Cheddar cheese and chives, and mix to combine. In a separate small bowl, place the cooking oil, milk, and egg yolk, and whisk to combine well. Create a well in the center of the dry ingredients, add the milk mixture, and mix to combine. Place the egg white in another clean, medium-size bowl, and beat with a handheld mixer on medium speed just until soft peaks form. Add the whipped egg white to the rest of the waffle batter in two batches, and fold in until no more than a few white streaks remain.

Open the preheated waffle iron, and pour about ¾ cup to 1 cup of batter on the waffle iron, depending upon the size of the waffle iron. Working quickly, spread the batter into an even layer, stopping about ¼ inch from the edge of the iron. Close and secure the lid, and allow the waffles to cook for about 4 minutes or until steam has largely stopped escaping from the iron. Open the iron, remove the waffles, and place on a wire rack to cool.

While the waffles are cooling, fry the chicken. Place paper towels on a plate, and set it aside. Place about 2 inches of oil in a medium-size, heavy-bottomed saucepan, and bring the oil to 350°F over medium-high heat. Remove the chicken pieces from the flour mixture and place them in batches in the hot oil, taking care not to crowd the oil. Fry for about 5 minutes or until lightly golden brown all over and cooked through. Remove the cooked chicken from the oil using a spider or a slotted spoon and place on the paper-towel-lined plate to drain. Bring the oil back to temperature between batches.

Assemble the chicken and waffles. Cut the cooled waffles into 2-inch-square pieces using a sharp knife or kitchen shears, and pair each waffle piece with a piece of fried chicken. Secure with a toothpick and serve.

MAKE-AHEAD OPTION: The waffles can easily be made ahead of time, cooled, wrapped tightly, and frozen before being cut into quarters. Defrost in the toaster oven on light. The chicken can be cut into pieces ahead of time, wrapped tightly, and frozen raw, then defrosted in the refrigerator overnight. The cooked chicken is best eaten right away but can be wrapped and stored in the refrigerator for up to 2 days, then gently reheated in a toaster oven.

NO-FRY OPTION: The chicken can be baked by placing the prepared pieces on an oven-safe wire rack positioned above a rimmed baking sheet. Spray the chicken generously with nonstick cooking spray, and bake at 375°F until lightly golden brown all over, about 15 minutes.

BIGGER BITE OPTION: Easy! Slice the chicken into strips instead of bite-size pieces and don't cut the waffles into quarters.

baked asparagus fries

ASPARAGUS FRIES ARE A FUN, CRUNCHY APPETIZER-worthy alternative to french fries, and they're actually straight-up healthy for you in a way that I'm afraid potatoes will never be. And they might just entice any family members who refuse to believe that these little green spears could ever be delicious to try them. The combination of mustard powder, paprika, and Parmesan cheese packs a lot of flavor into every spear. If you shy away from buying fresh asparagus because it goes bad before you have a chance to use it, see page 8 for my tips on storing to prolong its shelf life considerably. Once prepared, these are best eaten right away.

Preheat your oven to 400°F. Line a large rimmed baking sheet with unbleached parchment paper, place an oven-safe wire rack on top of the baking sheet, and set it aside. Wash the asparagus, trim any fibrous ends, and pat the spears very dry. Set them aside.

Set up a dipping station with three wide, flat bowls. In the first bowl, place the flour, salt, pepper, paprika, and mustard powder, and whisk to combine well. In the second bowl, place the eggs and milk, and beat to combine well. In the third bowl, place the breadcrumbs and Parmigiano-Reggiano cheese, and mix to combine. Dredge each asparagus spear through the flour blend, coating it on all sides, then in the egg wash, allowing any excess to drip off, and finally press into the breadcrumb mixture to help the breadcrumbs adhere on all sides. Place the prepared spears in a single layer about 1 inch apart from one another on the rack on top of the prepared baking sheet. Spray the tops of the asparagus spears on the baking sheet generously with the cooking oil spray.

Place the baking sheet in the preheated oven and bake for about 15 minutes or until the spears are golden brown and crispy. Remove from the oven and allow to cool briefly before serving.

MAKES 15 TO 20 FRIES

1 pound fresh asparagus

½ cup (70 g) Basic Gum-Free Gluten-Free Flour (page 4), plus more as necessary

½ teaspoon kosher salt

¼ teaspoon freshly ground black pepper

1 teaspoon smoked Spanish paprika

½ teaspoon mustard powder

2 eggs (100 g, weighed out of shell), at room temperature

2 tablespoons milk (any kind), at room temperature

2 cups (240 g) panko-style gluten-free breadcrumbs (page 216)

2 ounces Parmigiano-Reggiano cheese, finely grated

potato skins

MAKES ABOUT 16 SERVINGS

2 pounds russet potatoes, rinsed and dried

3 tablespoons (42 g) unsalted butter, melted

1 teaspoon kosher salt

⅛ teaspoon freshly ground black pepper

1 teaspoon garlic powder

4 ounces sharp yellow Cheddar cheese, shredded

Sour cream, for serving

2 tablespoons chopped fresh chives, for serving

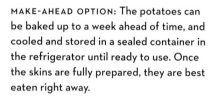

MAKE-AHEAD OPTION: The potatoes can be baked up to a week ahead of time, and cooled and stored in a sealed container in the refrigerator until ready to use. Once the skins are fully prepared, they are best eaten right away.

BIGGER BITE OPTION: Make with large Idaho potatoes! Baking time and time under the broiler will have to be increased.

WHEN ONE OF MY CHILDREN INSISTS THAT THEY don't like a particular food, a small part of me can't help but see it as something of a challenge to change his or her mind. Case in point: potatoes. My oldest child simply does not care for potatoes in most any form, even french fries (!). But when I serve her these crispy, crunchy, buttery, and cheesy potato skins, she finds them downright irresistible. Serve the larger bite option with a simple puréed soup and you can call it dinner!

Preheat your oven to 375°F. Line a large rimmed baking sheet with unbleached parchment paper, and set it aside.

Place a large piece of aluminum foil directly on the middle rack of the preheated oven, and place the potatoes on top in a single layer. Bake until the skins are crisp and the inside flesh of the potatoes begin to shrink away from the skin (the skins will wrinkle), about 45 minutes. Transfer the potatoes to a wire rack to cool briefly.

Using a sharp knife, slice each potato half lengthwise, scoop out most of the cooked potato inside the skin, leaving about ¼ inch of soft baked potato inside each skin, then set aside the cooked potato for another use (like Potato Croquettes, page 41).

Brush the insides of the potatoes lightly with the melted butter, then sprinkle evenly with salt, pepper, and garlic powder. Invert the potato skins, brush the outsides with the remaining butter, and season again with salt. Place the prepared potato skins, skin-side up, on the prepared baking sheet. Place under your oven's broiler, and bake until the skins begin to bubble and crisp, about 2 minutes. Re-invert the skins, divide the grated cheese among them, and return to the broiler for another 3 minutes, or until the inside edges of the skins have just begun to crisp and the cheese is melted and bubbling. Remove from the oven, and top each with a small dollop of sour cream and a few chopped chives. Serve immediately.

roasted chickpeas

ALTHOUGH FALAFEL (PAGE 37) HAS A SET OF RULES for preparing, when it comes to roasted chickpeas, it's OK to wing it. In fact, it's encouraged! As long as you drain, rinse, and pat dry canned chickpeas, and then allow them to dry some more in the open air, drizzle with olive oil, and salt them a bit, you really can't go wrong. I like the smoky-salty-fresh combination of salt, smoked paprika, and fresh parsley but feel free to substitute your favorite herbs and spices. In other words, the first three ingredients in this recipe are essential; the remaining ones are mere suggestions. Make it yours!

Preheat your oven to 375°F. Line a large rimmed baking sheet with unbleached parchment paper and set it aside.

Place the chickpeas on a large tea towel or a few paper towels, and pat dry gently. Allow the chickpeas to sit uncovered at room temperature for a few minutes to ensure that they are very dry, which will help them crisp in the oven. Place the dried chickpeas on the prepared baking sheet, toss with the olive oil and salt to coat completely, and spread into an even layer on the baking sheet. Place the baking sheet in the center of the preheated oven and bake for 15 minutes. Remove the pan from the oven, stir, return it to the oven, and continue to bake until the chickpeas are dark golden brown all over (another 10 to 15 minutes).

Sprinkle the paprika over the chickpeas and stir to coat evenly. Add the chopped parsley, and toss to coat. Serve immediately. They will crisp as they cool, but lose their crispness within about an hour.

MAKES 3 CUPS

2 15-ounce cans chickpeas, drained and rinsed

2 tablespoons (28 g) extra-virgin olive oil

1 teaspoon kosher salt, plus more to taste

1 teaspoon smoked paprika

2 teaspoons chopped fresh flat-leaf parsley

MAKE-AHEAD OPTION: Roasted chickpeas simply won't stay crisp for very long, even when stored in a sealed glass container. They can, however, be prepped ahead of time by allowing them to sit uncovered for a few hours, or even overnight, before roasting.

stuffed mushrooms

STUFFED MUSHROOMS ARE ALWAYS A CROWD FAVOR-ite, and luckily they're not time consuming to make. Made with a savory combination of onions, garlic, soy sauce, chopped arti-chokes, Parmigiano-Reggiano cheese, and goat cheese, the filling is packed with flavor. These baby stuffed mushrooms are gone in about two (small) bites, so make plenty! If you decide to go with the "Bigger Bite Option," try placing the stuffed, baked large portobello mushroom in a roll and serving as a sandwich, or slicing it into strips and serving over a salad.

MAKES 24 MUSHROOMS

24 large baby bella or button mushrooms

2 tablespoons (28 g) unsalted butter

1 small yellow onion, peeled and diced

2 garlic cloves, peeled and minced

1 tablespoon gluten-free soy sauce or
   tamari

½ cup (60 g) panko-style gluten-free
   breadcrumbs

1 can (14 ounces) artichoke hearts packed
   in water, drained and chopped

2 ounces Parmigiano-Reggiano cheese,
   finely grated

3 ounces goat cheese, crumbled

1 egg (50 g, weighed out of shell)

———— ⚓ ————

MAKE-AHEAD OPTION: The filling, without the goat cheese and egg, can be made up to 3 days ahead of time and stored in a sealed container in the refrigerator. Add the egg and crumbled goat cheese right before stuffing and baking the mushroom caps. Once baked, they can be eaten right away or stored in the refrigerator for a couple of days before being warmed gently in the oven or microwave and served.

BIGGER BITE OPTION: In place of small mushrooms, use large portobello mush-rooms for stuffing. Increase baking time to 20 to 25 minutes.

———— ⚓ ————

Preheat your oven to 350°F. Line a large rimmed baking sheet with parchment paper or greased aluminum foil and set it aside.

Clean the mushrooms by brushing with a damp paper towel or cloth. Remove and dice the stems, and set aside.

In a large skillet, heat the butter over medium heat until melted. Add the onion and cook, stirring occasionally, until translucent, about 5 minutes. Add the minced garlic and cook, stirring occasionally, until fragrant, about 1 minute more. Add the diced mushroom stems and mix to combine. Remove the pan from the heat and transfer to a large bowl. Add the soy sauce, breadcrumbs, and artichoke hearts, and mix to combine. Allow the mixture to cool briefly before adding the Parmigiano-Reggiano cheese, goat cheese, and egg, and mix gently to combine.

Place as much filling as will fit inside each of the mushroom caps, packing it tightly but taking care not to burst the caps. Place them about 1 inch apart from one another on the pre-pared baking sheet. Place the baking sheet in the center of the preheated oven and bake until the mushroom caps are golden brown and the filling is melted, about 15 minutes. Serve immediately.

corn muffin bites

THESE BUTTERY CORN MUFFIN BITES, STUDDED WITH kernels of fresh corn that pop in your mouth, are lightly sweetened with only a bit of honey. If you're serving them as an appetizer, try serving them with a small bowl of extra honey and a honey dipper for your guests to drizzle over their corn muffins before eating.

Preheat your oven to 350°F. Grease or line the wells of a 24-cup miniature muffin tin and set it aside.

In a large bowl, place the cornmeal, flour, baking powder, baking soda, and salt, and whisk to combine well. Add the corn kernels, and mix until evenly distributed throughout the dry ingredients. Create a well in the center of the dry ingredients and add the butter, honey, egg, and buttermilk, mixing to combine after each addition. The batter should be thick but soft. Divide the batter evenly among the prepared wells of the muffin tin. Place the tin in the center of the preheated oven and bake until a toothpick inserted into the center of the muffins comes out with no more than a few moist crumbs attached, about 15 minutes. Remove from the oven and allow to cool for at least 5 minutes in the muffin tin before transferring to a wire rack to cool completely.

MAKES 24 MUFFINS

1¼ cups (165 g) coarsely ground gluten-free yellow cornmeal

1 cup (140 g) all-purpose gluten-free flour (page 2)

1½ teaspoons baking powder

¼ teaspoon baking soda

½ teaspoon (3 g) kosher salt

4 ounces fresh or frozen corn kernels (if frozen, do not defrost)

6 tablespoons (84 g) unsalted butter, melted and cooled

3 tablespoons (63 g) honey

1 large egg (50 g, weighed out of shell), at room temperature, beaten

1¼ cups plus 2 tablespoons (11 fluid ounces) buttermilk, at room temperature

❦

MAKE-AHEAD OPTION: The batter for these muffins can be made up to a day ahead of time and stored in a sealed container in the refrigerator. The muffins can also be baked ahead of time, then sealed tightly in a freezer-safe container, and frozen for up to 2 months. Defrost at room temperature and toast lightly before serving to refresh.

BIGGER BITE OPTION: Make these minis into full muffins by baking them in a standard 12-cup muffin tin. Increase the baking time to about 22 minutes.

⚘

miniature cream cheese biscuits

MAKES ABOUT 18 MINIBISCUITS

2½ cups (350 g) Gluten-Free Pastry Flour (page 5), plus more for sprinkling

2 teaspoons baking powder

¼ teaspoon baking soda

1 teaspoon kosher salt

6 tablespoons (84 g) unsalted butter, roughly chopped and chilled

4 ounces cream cheese, chilled

¾ cup (6 fluid ounces) milk, chilled, plus more for brushing tops

MAKE-AHEAD OPTION: Biscuits of all kinds are perfect for preparing ahead of time. Simply freeze the raw, shaped biscuits in a single layer on a baking sheet and then pile into a freezer-safe bag. Seal the bag tightly, and freeze until ready to use. Place on a prepared baking sheet, and bake from frozen, keeping an eye on the baking time, as the frozen biscuits will likely need about another 3 to 5 minutes in the oven. Once baked, they are best eaten right away.

BIGGER BITE OPTION: Just cut your biscuits with a larger size biscuit cutter and increase the baking time by about 5 minutes, depending upon size.

ADDING CREAM CHEESE TO A BISCUIT IS ACTUALLY a way to replace some of the milk, not the butter. Cream cheese is more similar in consistency to buttermilk or milk than it is to butter, as it doesn't harden fully even when frozen. Like buttermilk in biscuits, the cream cheese adds moisture and tenderness to these biscuits and makes them ideal for serving in miniature as they can bake without risk of becoming too crispy. Since they bake up so soft, these biscuits are particularly well suited to being sliced in half and filled like tea sandwiches, with sliced cucumbers and cream cheese, sliced ham and brie cheese, or egg salad and watercress.

Preheat your oven to 375°F. Line a rimmed baking sheet with unbleached parchment paper and set it aside.

In a large bowl, place the flour, baking powder, baking soda, and salt, and whisk to combine well. Add the butter, separate the pieces, and toss in the dry ingredients. With clean, dry, well-floured fingers, flatten the flour-covered pieces of butter. Add the cream cheese, break it into pieces, and toss it in the dry ingredients.

Create a well in the center of the bowl, and add the milk. Stir gently to combine until the dough begins to come together. Turn the dough out onto a lightly floured piece of parchment paper, and pat it into a rectangle about ¼ inch thick. Dust the dough lightly with flour, and fold it in thirds by the short sides, like a business letter. Turn the dough one quarter of the way around in one direction, cover with another sheet of parchment paper, and roll out into a rectangle about ¼ inch thick.

Flour a 2½-inch round biscuit cutter; cut out rounds of dough and place them on the prepared baking sheet. Gather and reroll the scraps, sprinkle lightly with flour if the dough is sticky, and cut more rounds of dough. Brush the tops of the biscuits with a bit of milk. Place the baking sheet in the freezer for 10 minutes, or until firm.

Place the baking sheet in the center of the preheated oven and bake for about 15 minutes, or until lightly golden brown, rotating once during baking.

spinach dip

TRUE, THIS CREAMY, CRUNCHY SPINACH DIP ISN'T itself truly a small bite. But it tastes so much like the spinach dip made with the Lipton Onion Soup Mix recipe of yesteryear, and the only way that you can enjoy it is by dipping a piece of celery, a chip, or a cracker into it and then taking a (wait for it) small bite, so I believe it qualifies.

In a small bowl, place the onion powder, salt, cornstarch, sugar, and pepper, and whisk to combine well. Set the bowl aside. Cook the spinach according to the package directions. Place the cooked spinach in a tea towel or nut milk bag and squeeze it until as much of the moisture as possible has been removed. Set the spinach aside.

In a small, heavy-bottomed saucepan, heat the olive oil over medium heat. Add the minced onion and carrots, and cook, stirring frequently, until the onion is translucent and lightly browned, about 5 minutes. Remove the mixture from the heat and set it aside to cool briefly.

In a large bowl, place the mayonnaise, sour cream, Worcestershire sauce, and onion powder mixture, and whisk to combine well. Add the Parmigiano-Reggiano, celery, spinach, onion and carrot mixture, and minced garlic, and mix to combine. Cover the bowl and place in the refrigerator to chill for at least an hour and up to 3 days. Serve chilled with celery stalks and gluten-free chips or crackers for dipping.

MAKES 3 CUPS OF DIP

2 teaspoons onion powder
1 teaspoon kosher salt
1 tablespoon (9 g) cornstarch
1 tablespoon (12 g) sugar
⅛ teaspoon freshly ground black pepper
1 pound chopped frozen spinach
1 tablespoon (14 g) extra-virgin olive oil
1 small yellow onion, peeled and minced
2 medium carrots, peeled and shredded
⅓ cup (75 g) mayonnaise
1½ cups (336 g) sour cream
1½ teaspoons gluten-free Worcestershire sauce
2 ounces Parmigiano-Reggiano cheese, finely grated
2 stalks celery heart, finely chopped (about ¾ cup)
2 garlic cloves, peeled and minced
Celery stalks and gluten-free chips or crackers, for serving

MAKE-AHEAD OPTION: The dry ingredients in this spinach dip (onion powder, salt, cornstarch, sugar, salt, and pepper) can be mixed months ahead of time and placed in a sealed container then stored in a cool, dry place. The dip itself can be made ahead and refrigerated for up to 3 days before serving, and it is arguably better on the third day than on the first.

spinach balls

MAKES 24 BALLS

6 tablespoons (84 g) unsalted butter, melted and cooled

3 eggs (150 g, weighed out of shell), at room temperature, lightly beaten

6 ounces grated sharp Cheddar cheese

3 ounces Parmigiano-Reggiano cheese, finely grated

2 teaspoons dried oregano

16 ounces chopped frozen spinach, thawed and drained well

2 cups (240 g) panko-style gluten-free breadcrumbs

3 tablespoons (27 g) all-purpose gluten-free flour (page 2)

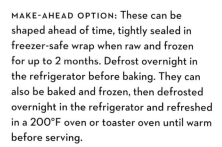

MAKE-AHEAD OPTION: These can be shaped ahead of time, tightly sealed in freezer-safe wrap when raw and frozen for up to 2 months. Defrost overnight in the refrigerator before baking. They can also be baked and frozen, then defrosted overnight in the refrigerator and refreshed in a 200°F oven or toaster oven until warm before serving.

BIGGER BITE OPTION: These can be shaped into 12 patties instead of 24 balls, and then baked as directed. You will need to watch the baking time, but it doesn't change much as the patties are larger, but not nearly as thick as the balls. When making them larger, try serving between two slices of bread.

EVEN THOUGH THIS RECIPE CALLS FOR A FULL POUND of spinach, and you can see it with your own eyes in the baked balls themselves, even spinach haters will rejoice in these buttery, cheesy delights. I know this because two of my three children fall into that category (spinach haters but spinach-ball lovers). The only labor-intensive part of the whole process is wringing the moisture out of the spinach, which can be done days ahead of time; store the spinach in a sealed container in the refrigerator.

Preheat your oven to 350°F. Line a large rimmed baking sheet with unbleached parchment paper and set it aside.

In a large bowl, place the butter and eggs, and mix until well combined. Add the Cheddar and Parmigiano-Reggiano cheeses, and mix to combine. Before adding the oregano, rub it in the palm of your hand to release the oils, and then add the spinach and breadcrumbs. Mix until it comes together. Add the flour, one tablespoon at a time, and incorporate into the mixture.

Roll the mixture into golf-ball-size balls, packing them tightly. Place 1 inch apart from one another on the prepared baking sheet. Place in the center of the preheated oven, and bake until the balls have begun to brown on the bottom and are cooked through, rotating once during baking, about 15 minutes. Serve immediately.

risotto cakes

I HAVE ALWAYS HAD TO MAKE A FRESH BATCH OF risotto for the purpose of making risotto cakes. There is one reason for that, and it's a good one: risotto is delicious, and I never have leftovers. If you are lucky enough to have some extra risotto lying around, by all means use it to make these creamy, delicious, and flavorful cakes. But if you're like me and leftover risotto just isn't going to happen, see below for Quick and Easy Risotto, the recipe that I like best for use in making risotto cakes. Just be sure to make the recipe in stages so you budget enough time for the cooked risotto to chill before making the cakes.

For the Quick and Easy Risotto: In a medium-size sauté pan, melt the butter and sauté the onion until translucent, about 6 minutes. Add the rice to the pan and cook, stirring frequently, until it becomes somewhat translucent, about 2 minutes. Add the wine and 2½ cups of the stock to the pan. Cook, stirring occasionally, until the liquid is mostly absorbed, about 10 minutes. Add the remaining stock, and continue to cook, stirring frequently, until the liquid is mostly absorbed again. Continue cooking, adding more water 2 tablespoons at a time as necessary, until the risotto is creamy. Add salt and pepper to taste. Allow the risotto to cool completely, then place in the refrigerator to chill.

For the Risotto Cakes: Line a rimmed baking sheet with unbleached parchment paper and set it aside. In a large bowl, place the risotto, Gruyère and Parmigiano-Reggiano cheeses, sour cream, lemon juice, egg whites, salt, paprika, and parsley, and mix carefully to combine without breaking up the risotto. Cover the bowl with plastic wrap and place in the refrigerator to chill for at least 10 minutes, or up to overnight.

Remove the chilled mixture and, with wet hands, divide it into disks about 1½ inches in diameter and about ¾ inch to 1 inch thick, pressing them firmly together. Press each disk in the breadcrumbs to coat generously, and then place it on the prepared baking sheet. Place the risotto cakes in the refrigerator to chill for at least 30 minutes, or up to overnight.

Place paper towels on a plate, and set it aside. In a large, heavy-bottomed skillet, heat 2 tablespoons of oil until it shimmers. Working in batches as necessary to avoid crowding the

MAKES 20 CAKES

FOR THE QUICK AND EASY RISOTTO

2 tablespoons (28 g) unsalted butter
1 small yellow onion, peeled and diced
1 cup uncooked risotto rice
¼ cup (2 fluid ounces) dry white wine (like pinot grigio)
3½ cups (28 fluid ounces) warm vegetable or chicken stock, divided
Kosher salt and freshly ground black pepper, to taste

FOR THE RISOTTO CAKES

2 cups cooked risotto, chilled
4 ounces Gruyère cheese, shredded
½ ounce Parmigiano-Reggiano cheese, finely grated
6 ounces sour cream
Juice of 1 lemon
2 egg whites (50 g)
½ teaspoon kosher salt, or more to taste
½ teaspoon smoked paprika
2 tablespoons finely chopped fresh parsley (or 1 tablespoon dried)
1½ cups (180 g) panko-style gluten-free breadcrumbs, plus more as necessary
Neutral oil, for frying

pan, place the risotto cakes in the hot oil and allow to cook, undisturbed, until a thin brown crust forms on the underside, about 5 minutes. Carefully turn each cake over and cook until a similar crust forms on the other side. Remove from the oil and place on the paper-towel-lined plate to drain. Repeat with any remaining risotto cakes and serve immediately.

MAKE-AHEAD OPTION: These can be made and shaped ahead of time, but not breaded, and then frozen in a single layer on a baking sheet. Pile the frozen risotto cakes into a freezer-safe bag and place in the freezer until ready to use. Defrost at room temperature before breading and frying. Once fully prepared, they are best eaten right away.

NO-FRY OPTION: The risotto cakes can be shaped, then breaded and baked instead of fried. Preheat your oven to 350°F and line a large rimmed baking sheet with unbleached parchment paper. Place the breaded risotto cakes on the baking sheet about 1 inch apart from one another, brush sparingly with an egg wash (1 egg beaten with 1 tablespoon water), and bake until lightly golden brown all over, about 20 minutes. Serve warm.

BIGGER BITE OPTION: Double the recipe and make the portions twice as large. Frying time will need to be increased by about another 3 minutes total.

cheesy potato pierogi

THERE ARE PLENTY OF DUMPLING-STYLE RECIPES IN this book, but pierogi are different from any other. Perhaps because most people's first experience with them is with a potato filling, or perhaps because there's sour cream right there in the dough, they're the stuff of warm, comforting memories. I didn't grow up eating pierogi, but traditions have to begin somewhere, so I intend to start my own. My children love them any way I prepare them (even with a slightly sweet blueberry filling, or stuffed with the Spinach Dip from page 75), but I think potato is our favorite. They're meant to be served warm with some sour cream on the side, but we also love them cold right from the refrigerator.

To make the dough, in a large bowl, place the sour cream, milk, egg, and salt, and whisk to combine well. Add the flour in three parts, mixing well to combine after each addition. The dough will come together and be relatively smooth but still a bit sticky. Turn the dough out onto a lightly floured surface and, with floured hands, knead the dough until it becomes easier to handle (it will not be completely smooth). Cover the dough loosely with plastic wrap, and set it aside to rest.

To make the filling, place the potatoes, with the skins still on, in a large pot and cover with cold, salted water by about 2 inches. Cover the pot, bring to a boil over medium heat, and allow to cook for about 30 minutes, or until the potatoes are fork-tender. Remove from the heat and drain the water. While the potatoes are still warm, remove the skins and pass the potatoes through a ricer or food mill or mash completely with a fork then place in a large bowl. Place the diced onion and clarified butter in a small skillet and cook over medium heat, stirring frequently, until the onions are translucent, about 6 minutes. To the potatoes, add the cooked onions, then the sour cream, shredded cheeses, and the salt and pepper to taste. Set the filling aside.

To shape the dough, place it on a lightly floured surface and roll it out into a round about ¼ inch thick, moving it frequently and dusting lightly with flour to prevent it from sticking as you roll. Cut out rounds 4 inches in diameter from the dough. Gather and reroll scraps. Roll each round into an oval that is closer to ⅛ inch thick (the thickness of a nickel).

MAKES 24 PIEROGI

FOR THE DOUGH

½ cup (112 g) sour cream, at room temperature
⅔ cup (5⅓ fluid ounces) milk, at room temperature
1 egg (50 g, weighed out of shell), at room temperature, beaten
⅛ teaspoon kosher salt
2½ cups (350 g) all-purpose gluten-free flour (page 2), plus more for sprinkling

FOR THE FILLING

1 pound potatoes (about 8 small red-skin potatoes or 1 large russet potato)
1 small onion, peeled and diced
2 tablespoons (28 g) clarified butter or ghee
½ cup (112 g) sour cream, at room temperature
1 ounce Monterey Jack cheese, shredded
1 ounce sharp Cheddar cheese, shredded
Kosher salt and freshly ground black pepper, to taste

FOR FINISHING

Egg wash (1 egg beaten with 1 tablespoon water)
2 tablespoons ghee or clarified butter

To assemble the pierogi, using a pastry brush, paint the edges of each oval with the egg wash, then place about 1 tablespoon of filling in the center of each. Fold the dough over on itself, matching the edges, and pushing out any trapped air. Pinch the edges together to form a tight seal. In a large pot of salted, boiling water, place the pierogi, about 6 at a time, until they float to the surface, about 3 minutes. Place the boiled pierogi on a paper towel to drain, then blot them dry. Eat immediately, or finish by sautéing the towel-dried pierogi in ghee in a large skillet until browned, about 2 minutes per side. Serve immediately.

MAKE-AHEAD OPTION: Follow the directions through boiling and drying the pierogi. Wrap the boiled dumplings tightly in freezer-safe wrap and freeze. Defrost overnight in the refrigerator until ready to serve. Finish with the sauté immediately before serving. Pierogi are, of course, delicious when served immediately after cooking but store very well in a sealed container in the refrigerator. Heat through before serving, or enjoy them cold.

garlic pizza breadsticks

1 recipe Thin Crust Pizza Dough (page 214)

4 garlic cloves, peeled and minced

½ teaspoon kosher salt

4 tablespoons (56 g) unsalted butter, melted

1 ounce finely grated Parmigiano-Reggiano cheese

8 ounces part-skim mozzarella cheese, grated

———— ⚓ ————

MAKE-AHEAD OPTION: The pizza dough can be made up to 5 days ahead of time and stored in a well-sealed proofing bucket or other secure container in the refrigerator. Shaping and baking the dough should be done right before serving.

BIGGER BITE OPTION: Just slice the baked crust into larger pieces!

———— ⚓ ————

THESE AREN'T YOUR TRADITIONAL ROUND BREAD-sticks, but instead are thin slices of delightfully garlicky white pizza. Brushing the dough with melted butter instead of olive oil, then scattering plenty of minced garlic all over the dough, makes for quite a treat. Serve them with tomato sauce for dipping or on their own for a guaranteed crowd-pleasing appetizer.

Make the pizza dough according to the recipe instructions and place the dough in a sealed container or bowl in a warm, draft-free location to rise until nearly doubled in size (1 to 2 hours, depending upon environment). Full doubling is not necessary. Place the risen dough, still in a sealed container or bowl, in the refrigerator to chill until firmer, about 30 minutes.

Place a pizza stone (or overturned rimmed metal baking sheet) on the bottom rack of your oven and preheat the oven to 400°F. On a lightly floured surface, knead the pizza dough until smoother. Roll the dough into a ball. Sprinkle lightly with flour, and, using well-floured hands and a rolling pin as necessary, pat and roll out the dough on a lightly floured surface into an oval shape, about 15 inches by 12 inches, rotating the dough and flouring it frequently, to prevent sticking. Transfer the round of dough to a piece of unbleached parchment paper.

Using the flat side of a large knife, press the minced garlic and salt together firmly to form a thick paste. Add the garlic paste to the melted butter, and mix to combine. Using a pastry brush, brush the entire surface of the pizza dough with the entire garlic butter mixture, all the way to the edges of the dough. Sprinkle evenly with the grated Parmigiano-Reggiano cheese, followed by the grated mozzarella cheese, all the way to the edge of the dough.

Place the crust, still on the parchment paper, on the hot pizza stone or inverted pan. Bake until the crust is browned and the cheese is melted and browned in spots (about 10 minutes, but time will vary depending upon how crisp you'd like the crust). Allow to set briefly before slicing down the length in the center and then across into sticks, 12 sticks per side, and serving.

pizza bites

PIZZA BITES ARE NOTHING MORE THAN SAUCE AND cheese wrapped in a bit of pizza dough, but they have that pop-in-your-mouth charm that makes them perfect for an after-school snack or a game-day appetizer.

Make the pizza dough according to the recipe instructions and place the dough in a sealed container or bowl in a warm, draft-free location to rise until nearly doubled in size (1 to 2 hours, depending upon environment). Full doubling is not necessary. Place the risen dough, still in a sealed container or bowl, in the refrigerator to chill until firmer, about 30 minutes. Alternatively, set the dough to rise in a sealed container in the refrigerator for about 12 hours or up to 5 days.

Preheat your oven to 375°F. Line rimmed baking sheets with unbleached parchment paper, and set them aside.

Once the dough has chilled, turn it out onto a lightly floured surface, sprinkle it lightly with more flour, and roll it into a smooth ball. Divide the dough into two equal pieces. Cover one with a moist tea towel and set it aside. Take the remaining half of dough and roll it out into a large rectangle about ¼ inch thick, sprinkling with flour as necessary. With a pastry or pizza wheel or a sharp knife, cut the rolled-out dough into 18 rectangles, each about 3 inches long by 1½ inches wide. Gather and reroll scraps as necessary.

Place about 1 teaspoon of tomato sauce on one half of each rectangle, leaving at least an ⅛-inch edge clean. Place 3 to 4 pieces of chopped cheese (less if the cheese is cut into a larger dice) on top of the sauce. Do not overfill. Fold the clean half of the rectangle over the sauce and cheese, press the edges together firmly to seal, and place the pizza bites about 1 inch apart from one another on the prepared baking sheet. Repeat with the remaining portion of dough.

Place the baking sheets in the center of the preheated oven, one at a time, and bake for 10 minutes. Remove the baking sheet from the oven, then quickly and carefully turn over each of the pizza bites. Return the baking sheet to the oven, and bake for another 7 minutes, or until the cheese is bubbling and the pizza bites are uniformly golden brown all over. Serve warm.

MAKES 36 BITES

1 recipe Thin Crust Pizza Dough
   (page 214)
½ cup (4 fluid ounces) thick tomato sauce
4 ounces Asiago (or other semihard)
   cheese, diced

MAKE-AHEAD OPTION: These bites can be made ahead, frozen in a single layer on a baking sheet, and then wrapped tightly in freezer-safe wrap and frozen until ready to use. Defrost at room temperature, in the microwave on 60% power, or in a 250°F oven until warmed throughout.

BIGGER BITE OPTION: Rather than making 1½-inch pizza bites, cut the dough into larger pieces and otherwise follow the recipe instructions. Increase baking time as necessary.

pizza pinwheels

MAKES 8 PINWHEELS

1 recipe Thin Crust Pizza Dough
(page 214)

Egg wash (1 egg beaten with 1 tablespoon
milk)

8 ounces part-skim mozzarella cheese,
shredded

2 ounces finely grated Parmigiano-
Reggiano cheese

6 ounces gluten-free pepperoni, chopped

Tomato sauce, for serving

———————— ❧ ————————

BIGGER BITE OPTION: Rather than slicing
the pinwheels into 2-inch-thick slices, simply slice them larger and bake for longer.

———————— ⚘ ————————

THESE CHEESY, SMOKY LITTLE BITES, FILLED WITH mozzarella, Parmigiano-Reggiano, and chopped pepperoni, make a much more dramatic presentation than just a plain old slice of pizza. Although they can't be made ahead, the ingredients can be gathered, and the pizza dough made up to 5 days in advance and stored in the refrigerator until you're ready for it. Once baked, these are best eaten right away.

Make the pizza dough according to the recipe instructions and place the dough in a sealed container or bowl in a warm, draft-free location to rise until nearly doubled in size (1 to 2 hours, depending upon environment). Full doubling is not necessary. Place the risen dough, still in a sealed container or bowl, in the refrigerator to chill until firmer, about 30 minutes. Alternatively, set the dough to rise in a sealed container in the refrigerator for about 12 hours or up to 5 days.

Once the dough has chilled, divide it into two equal pieces. Cover one with a moist tea towel and set it aside. Take the remaining half of dough and roll it into a 8 x 6-inch rectangle, dusting lightly with flour to prevent sticking or tearing. Brush the surface of the dough evenly with the egg wash. Scatter half of the mozzarella cheese, then half of the Parmigiano-Reggiano cheese, and half of the chopped pepperoni evenly across the surface, leaving a ½-inch border clean all around. Press gently to adhere the topping to the dough. Beginning at a long end and rolling away from you, roll up the dough like a jelly roll, ending with the roll seam-side down. With a sharp knife or pizza wheel, slice the dough into 2-inch-thick slices by cross-section, and lay the slices, cut-side down, on the prepared baking sheet, two inches apart. Repeat with the remaining half of the dough and other ingredients.

Place the baking sheets in the center of the preheated oven, one at a time, and bake until golden brown all over, about 15 minutes. Remove from the oven and allow the cheese to set for 5 minutes before serving warm, with tomato sauce.

miniature mac and cheese cups

THERE ARE TWO BASIC STYLES OF MACARONI AND cheese: custard style and cheese-sauce style. Custard style is more like a casserole, as it contains eggs and must be baked. Cheese-sauce style is essentially a cheese sauce made from a flour roux, folded into boiled pasta, and served immediately. These mac and cheese cups are a hybrid of sorts, as they're made with a gorgeous mozzarella and Cheddar cheese sauce but with the addition of one egg—just enough to help the cups hold together beautifully when they're baked but not so much that they bake up like miniature casseroles. The best of both mac and cheese worlds! Plus, they freeze and reheat perfectly.

Boil the pasta in a large pasta pot to an al dente texture, according to the package directions. Drain the pasta, return it to the pot, and toss it with olive oil to prevent it from sticking together. Cover the pot and set it aside.

Preheat your oven to 375°F. Generously grease the wells of two 12-cup standard muffin tins, and set them aside.

To make the cheese sauce, melt the chopped butter in a medium-size, heavy-bottomed saucepan over medium heat. Add the flour and whisk to combine well. The mixture will clump at first, and then smooth after it cooks for a minute or so. This is the roux that will thicken the cheese sauce. Cook over medium heat, stirring constantly, until the mixture has just begun to turn a very light-brown color, about 2 minutes. Add the evaporated milk to the roux very slowly, stirring constantly to break up any lumps that might form. Add 1 cup of milk, and whisk to combine well. Bring the mixture to a simmer, and continue to cook, stirring occasionally, until thickened and reduced by about one-quarter, about 7 minutes. The sauce should coat the back of a spoon. Remove the saucepan from the heat, add the shredded cheeses, salt, and pepper, and mix to combine. The cheese sauce should be very thickly pourable. Add the beaten egg to the remaining milk, and pour the mixture into the cheese sauce, mixing constantly. Pour the hot cheese sauce over the cooked pasta, and stir carefully to coat all of the pasta in the cheese sauce without breaking up the pasta at all.

8 ounces small dried gluten-free pasta (like elbows)

1 to 2 tablespoons (14 to 28 g) extra-virgin olive oil

2 tablespoons (28 g) unsalted butter, chopped

3 tablespoons (27 g) Basic Gum-Free Gluten-Free Flour (page 4)

6 fluid ounces (½ can) evaporated milk

1 to 1¼ cups (8 to 10 fluid ounces) milk, at room temperature

4 ounces part-skim mozzarella cheese, shredded

4 ounces sharp yellow Cheddar cheese, shredded

¼ teaspoon kosher salt

⅛ teaspoon freshly ground black pepper

1 egg (50 g, weighed out of shell), at room temperature, beaten

MAKE-AHEAD OPTION: These mac and cheese cups can be baked ahead of time. Cool the cups completely, then freeze them in a single layer on a baking sheet before sealing them, frozen, in freezer-safe wrap and returning them to the freezer. Defrost at room temperature, and reheat them in a microwave oven before serving. If you don't have a microwave, you can reheat them in the oven. Place the cups on a lined baking sheet and preheat your oven to 300°F. Sprinkle them each with a few drops of water and place them in the preheated oven for about 10 minutes or until warm. Do not overbake.

BIGGER BITE OPTION: Rather than baking this mac and cheese as individual cups, it can be placed in a greased 12 x 9-inch baking dish and baked at 350°F until lightly golden brown all over and set, about 35 minutes.

Fill the prepared wells of the miniature muffin tins just past the top with the macaroni and cheese mixture, and press down carefully but firmly to pack the mixture into the well. Place the muffin tins, one at a time, in the center of the preheated oven. Bake for about 15 minutes or until the tops are golden brown. Remove from the oven and allow to cool in the muffin tins for 5 minutes before running a toothpick around the edge of each muffin well to loosen the cups and popping them out. Serve warm.

spanakopita bites

IF YOU HAVE FOND MEMORIES OF EATING SPANAKO-pita, making it yourself is pretty much the only way you are going to get to eat it gluten-free. I won't tell you that it's no trouble at all to make, but I will tell you that this homemade gluten-free version bakes up just like you remember and that it's all worth it in the end. As soon as you bite through the layers of crispy baked phyllo dough into that soft, warm spinach and feta cheese combination, you'll know. When working with the homemade phyllo dough, if you're not certain whether you should continue to roll it thinner, go ahead and roll it one more time. Use the photos as a guide. Made as a pie according to the "Bigger Bite" instructions, this recipe makes a luxurious main dish when served with a dollop of thick yogurt and a Greek salad.

MAKES ABOUT 16 BITES

1 tablespoon (14 g) extra-virgin olive oil
1 medium shallot, peeled and diced
16 ounces fresh spinach (or frozen whole leaf spinach, defrosted)
4 ounces feta cheese, crumbled
1 large egg, at room temperature
⅛ teaspoon kosher salt
⅛ teaspoon freshly ground black pepper
½ recipe Phyllo Dough (page 194)
2 to 4 tablespoons (28 to 56 g) unsalted butter, melted

Preheat your oven to 350°F. Line a large rimmed baking sheet with unbleached parchment paper, and set it aside.

In a heavy-bottomed saucepan, heat the olive oil over medium heat. Add the diced shallot and cook, stirring occasionally, until translucent, about 4 minutes. Remove the cooked shallot from the pan and set aside. Add the fresh spinach, and cook, stirring occasionally, until wilted. Remove from the heat and allow to cool. Once cool, place the spinach in a clean tea towel or strong paper towels, and wring out until all water has been removed. Chop the cooked, dry spinach roughly, and place in the medium-size bowl with the cooked shallot, feta cheese, egg, salt, and pepper, and mix to combine. Set the filling aside.

Place 1 sheet of fresh phyllo dough on a lightly floured surface, with the short side of the rectangle facing you. Sprinkle lightly with more flour, and using a sharp knife, pastry wheel, or pizza cutter, cut the rectangle in half lengthwise so you have two equal rectangles, each about 10 inches by 4 inches. Separate the rectangles and roll each away from you so that it is about 11 inches by 4 inches (or as long as you can make it without the dough tearing). The dough should be nearly translucent. Brush each rectangle generously with melted butter. About ½ inch from the bottom of each rectangle, place about 1 tablespoon of filling. Pull one of the bottom corners of the rectangle of dough up over the filling on an angle (toward the opposite side of the dough) to make a triangle. Brush the top of the triangle with more melted butter, and fold it over on itself

again toward the other side of the dough rectangle. Brush again with melted butter, and continue to fold the dough, brushing with melted butter each time, until you reach the top of the rectangle. Repeat with the other piece of dough, and then more sheets of phyllo dough and filling. Place the spanakopita on the prepared baking sheet, about 1 inch apart from one another. Place the baking sheet in the center of the preheated oven and bake until lightly golden brown all over, about 20 minutes. Remove from the oven and serve immediately.

MAKE-AHEAD OPTION: The filling can be made up to 3 days ahead and stored in a sealed container in the refrigerator until ready to use. The phyllo dough can also be made ahead and frozen flat on a baking sheet, then sealed in freezer-safe wrap and frozen again. Defrost in the refrigerator before using. Once baked, these flaky bites are best eaten right away.

BIGGER BITE OPTION: To make a spanakopita pie, line a 12 x 9-inch rimmed baking sheet with unbleached parchment paper. Place one sheet of phyllo dough in the bottom of the pan and brush with melted butter; follow with another sheet and brush with melted butter, then a third sheet, and brush again with melted butter. Scrape the spinach mixture into the pan and spread into an even layer. Top with the remaining sheets of phyllo dough, brushing each with melted butter before placing the next sheet of phyllo on top, ending with a layer of melted butter. Place the baking sheet in a preheated 350°F oven and bake until lightly golden brown all over, about 25 minutes. Remove from the oven and allow to cool for 10 minutes or until set before slicing into squares and serving.

chapter 5:
bigger bites: wraps & roll-ups

cheesesteak wraps

IF YOU'RE THE SORT OF PERSON WHO THINKS THAT a cheesesteak isn't a cheesesteak unless it's served on a hoagie roll, then you'll want to skip to the next recipe. Wrap this classic combination of quickly cooked, thinly sliced steak with mushrooms, onions, and perfect melty cheese in a flour tortilla, and you will transform a cheesesteak into finger food that can be eaten on the way to and from wherever your busy life takes you, all without making a mess.

Remove the steak from the freezer, and slice it width-wise (against the grain), as thinly as you can manage. If your husband is not from Philly, then however you slice it will be fine. Just give it your best shot. Sprinkle ¼ teaspoon salt evenly over the slices.

In a large sauté pan with high sides (or a large Dutch oven), heat 2 tablespoons of oil over medium-high heat. Carefully place some of the slices of steak in the pan in a single layer, making sure they don't overlap. Sauté for a minute, and then flip the slices with tongs. Cook for another minute or so, and remove the cooked slices from the pan. Repeat with the remaining slices, being careful not to overcrowd the pan. Set the beef aside.

Once all the steak has been cooked, add the remaining two tablespoons of oil and the onion to the pan. Lower the heat a bit. Cook, stirring frequently, until the onions are translucent but have not yet begun to brown, about 6 minutes. Remove the onions from the pan, and set them aside in their own separate bowl.

Add the sliced mushrooms to the same pan, so they can cook in the onion and beef juices. Add the remaining ¼ teaspoon of salt and stir to combine. Raise the heat again to medium high, and cover the pot for about 3 to 4 minutes to sweat the mushrooms. Uncover the pot and cook, stirring occasionally, until the mushrooms are soft and fragrant, about another 4 minutes. Remove the mushrooms from the pan and place them in their own separate bowl, as well.

Assemble the cheesesteaks. Divide the beef among the tortillas in the center of each, adding the (optional) mushrooms and (not really optional) onions, top with the slices of cheese, fold in the sides slightly, and roll away from yourself into a cylinder, burrito style. The warm beef and onions will melt the thinly sliced cheese. Slice in half by cross-section and serve immediately. Alternatively, serve open-faced.

MAKES 6 WRAPS

1½ pounds (24 ounces) steak (rib-eye, eye roll, or flank steak work well), frozen for about an hour before slicing

½ teaspoon kosher salt, divided

4 tablespoons (56 g) neutral oil (like canola or vegetable oil), divided

1 large yellow onion, peeled and diced

10 ounces white mushrooms, cleaned and sliced thinly (optional)

½ pound block of cheese (American or provolone work best), sliced thinly

6 8-inch Flour Tortillas, warmed in a hot, dry skillet until flexible (page 198)

MAKE-AHEAD OPTION: All of the component parts of these wraps can easily be prepared ahead of time (the steak, onions, and mushrooms all cooked and placed in separate containers, the cheese sliced, the tortillas made). Just quickly reheat the beef, onions, and mushrooms in a sauté pan before assembling and serving.

greek salad wraps

MAKES 6 WRAPS

3 garlic cloves, peeled and minced

1 tablespoon white wine vinegar

8 ounces Greek-style plain yogurt

1 tablespoon (14 g) extra-virgin olive oil

1 tablespoon chopped fresh dill

1 tablespoon freshly squeezed lemon juice

1½ pounds skinless, boneless chicken
   breasts

6 8-inch Flour Tortillas (page 198), warmed
   in a dry skillet until flexible

½ cup hummus

1 cup chopped romaine lettuce

1 cup chopped cucumber

4 ounces feta cheese, crumbled

¼ cup kalamata olives, pitted and roughly
   chopped

———————— ⚜ ————————

MAKE-AHEAD OPTION: The chicken can
be made ahead of time and refrigerated
in a sealed container for up to 3 days (or
frozen for longer; defrost overnight in the
refrigerator), then reheated in a bit of oil
in a warm skillet before assembling the
rest of the wraps and serving.

———————— ⚜ ————————

THINK OF THESE GREEK SALAD WRAPS LIKE ALL THE
best parts of a Greek salad (feta, olives, garlic, vinaigrette)
wrapped up with hummus in a warm, soft flour tortilla. They make
for a light and refreshing warm-weather meal, or each wrap can
be sliced into 4 portions by cross-section, each portion secured
with a toothpick. They make great game-day finger foods or
appetizers that way.

Make the sauce and marinate the chicken. In a large bowl,
place the garlic, vinegar, yogurt, olive oil, dill, and lemon juice,
and whisk to combine well. Transfer the sauce to a large, zip-top
bag. Place the chicken in the bag and close it. Massage the
outside of the bag gently to ensure that the sauce is marinating
all of the chicken. Place the bagged chicken in the refrigerator
for at least 1 hour and up to 1 day.

Cook the chicken. Line a large rimmed baking sheet with
heavy-duty aluminum foil and spray lightly with cooking oil
spray. Remove the chicken from the marinade and place in a
single, even layer on the prepared baking sheet. Discard the
remaining sauce. Turn on your oven's broiler and place the
baking sheet about 4 inches from the flame. Broil for 6 minutes.
Remove the pan from the oven, flip the chicken breasts over
with a fork, and return to the broiler for another 4 to 6 minutes,
or until the chicken is cooked through. Remove the chicken
from the oven and allow to cool for about 5 minutes before
cutting it into cubes.

Assemble the wraps. Place one flour tortilla on a flat surface, and spread one side evenly with about 2 tablespoons of
hummus. Place about ⅙ of the cubed chicken in the center of
the tortilla, then add about ⅙ of the chopped lettuce, chopped
cucumber, feta cheese, and olives, and press gently so the filling
adheres. Fold the bottom of the tortilla over the filling, folding
away from yourself, then fold the sides in about one-quarter
of the way and roll the rest of the tortilla away from yourself
tightly to seal. Slice in half by cross-section. Repeat with the
remaining wraps and other ingredients. Serve immediately.

california wraps

THE CREAMY BUTTERMILK AND SOUR CREAM MIXED with the light bite of finely minced raw garlic in the dressing for these wraps is worth the price of admission alone. In fact, my children will eat nearly anything if it's drizzled with ranch dressing. Since I often serve turkey sandwiches for lunch, the extra touches of ranch dressing, avocado, and bean sprouts, plus serving them on tortillas, are what make these wraps a welcome on-the-go meal. They're also lovely served as pinwheel appetizers when sliced in cross-section.

Make the dressing. In the bowl of a blender or food processor, place all of the dressing ingredients and blend or process until very smooth.

    Assemble the wraps. Place one flour tortilla on a flat surface and spread one side evenly with about 2 tablespoons of ranch dressing. Place about 2 ounces of the turkey, ¼ cup of the tomatoes, one-quarter of the cubed avocado, and ½ ounce of the bean sprouts on top, and press gently so the filling adheres. Fold the bottom of the tortilla over the filling, folding away from yourself, then fold the sides in about one-quarter of the way and roll the rest of the tortilla away from yourself tightly to seal. Repeat with the remaining wraps and other ingredients. Slice each in half by cross-section and serve immediately. Alternatively, serve open-faced.

MAKE-AHEAD OPTION: The ranch dressing can be made ahead of time and stored in a sealed container in the refrigerator for at least a week, or until the dairy ingredients spoil, which will depend upon their freshness when the dressing is made.

crispy chicken and slaw wraps

MAKES 6 WRAPS

⅓ cup (85 g) mayonnaise

⅓ cup (85 g) plain yogurt

1 tablespoon white wine vinegar

3 tablespoons (42 g) extra-virgin olive oil

1 tablespoon (12 g) granulated sugar

¼ teaspoon kosher salt

1 small red onion, peeled and chopped

10 ounces shredded green cabbage

1 pound skinless, boneless chicken breasts, thinly sliced

6 8-inch Flour Tortillas (page 198), warmed in a hot, dry skillet until flexible

6 ounces sharp yellow Cheddar cheese, shredded

———— ⚜ ————

MAKE-AHEAD OPTION: The chicken can be made ahead of time and refrigerated for up to 2 days or frozen, then defrosted overnight in the refrigerator. The coleslaw can also be made ahead of time, up to 2 days, and kept in a sealed container in the refrigerator. Once assembled, these wraps are best eaten right away.

———— ⚜ ————

LET'S GET SOMETHING CLEARED UP RIGHT AWAY: THE chicken in these wraps is pretty much the only thing that isn't crispy. The crispness comes from the perfectly dressed slaw and the wraps themselves, which are cooked in a hot skillet after they're assembled. If you consider yourself the sort of person who doesn't care for coleslaw, I hope you'll reserve judgment until you try this recipe. Made with a mix of mayonnaise and plain yogurt, it's in a class by itself.

Make the coleslaw. In a large bowl, place the mayonnaise, yogurt, vinegar, oil, sugar, and salt, and whisk until well combined. Place half of the yogurt mixture in a large bowl, add the onion and shredded cabbage on top, and toss to coat well. Cover and chill at least 1 hour before serving.

Place the remaining yogurt mixture in a large, zip-top bag, and then place the skinless, boneless chicken breasts in the bag. Close the bag tightly and massage the chicken gently to coat it completely. Place in the refrigerator to marinate for 1 hour or up to 2 days. Remove the chicken from the marinade and place side by side on a rimmed baking sheet lined with aluminum foil and greased with cooking spray. Discard any remaining marinade.

Place the chicken directly under your oven's broiler and cook for 6 minutes. Remove the chicken from the oven and flip each breast over carefully. Return to the oven and broil until cooked through (4 to 6 minutes more, depending upon the thickness of the chicken). Remove the chicken from the oven and allow to rest for at least 5 minutes before slicing each breast into strips.

Assemble the wraps. Place one flour tortilla on a flat surface and place about one-sixth of the shredded cheese down the center. Top with about one-sixth of the chicken strips, and then about one-sixth of the coleslaw, pressing gently so the filling adheres. Roll the tortilla to close, leaving the edges open. Repeat with the remaining tortillas and filling.

Spray the filled tortillas with cooking oil and heat a greased cast-iron (or nonstick) skillet over medium-high heat (medium low if using a nonstick skillet). Place the tortillas two at a time, seam-side down, on the hot skillet and for about 2 minutes per side, or until lightly golden brown all over. Repeat with the remaining filled tortillas. Serve immediately.

chicken caesar salad wraps

1 pound skinless, boneless chicken breasts

2 tablespoons (28 g) extra virgin olive oil

½ teaspoon kosher salt, divided

¼ teaspoon freshly ground black pepper, divided

¾ cup (168 g) mayonnaise

1 ounce Parmigiano-Reggiano cheese, chopped or grated

2 small garlic cloves, peeled and roughly chopped

3 tablespoons freshly squeezed lemon juice

1 teaspoon gluten-free fish sauce, gluten-free Worcestershire sauce, or anchovy paste

Milk or buttermilk by the ½ teaspoonful, as necessary

6 ounces romaine lettuce, chopped or torn into bite-size pieces

6 8-inch Flour Tortillas (page 198), warmed in a hot, dry skillet until flexible

MAKE-AHEAD OPTION: The chicken can be made ahead of time and refrigerated for up to 2 days or frozen, then defrosted overnight in the refrigerator. The salad can also be made ahead of time, up to 2 days, and kept in a sealed container in the refrigerator. The dressing can be made ahead of time and stored in a sealed container in the refrigerator for up to a week, if not more (depending upon the freshness of your ingredients).

DO YOURSELF A FAVOR AND DOUBLE THE CAESAR salad dressing in this recipe. You're gonna want to serve these wraps with extra dressing—and then to dress everything else you can think of with it. If you have another way you love to cook chicken breasts for shredded chicken, or you're pressed for time and want to use a gluten-free rotisserie chicken, don't let me stand in your way. Since they're wrapped up tightly like burritos, they're ready to head out the door whenever you are.

Cook the chicken. Preheat your oven to 400°F. Place the chicken breasts about 1 inch apart from one another in a 12 x 9-inch baking dish. Drizzle the chicken breasts with olive oil, then sprinkle with ¼ teaspoon salt and ⅛ teaspoon pepper. Spray the underside of a large piece of parchment paper, large enough to cover the whole baking dish, with cooking oil, and place, oiled-side down, directly on top of the chicken breasts in the pan. Place the pan in the oven and bake until the chicken reaches 165°F on an instant-read thermometer, about 30 minutes. Remove the chicken from the oven and shred with two forks while it's still warm. Place the shredded chicken in a large bowl and set it aside.

Make the dressing and filling. In a blender, place the mayonnaise, Parmigiano-Reggiano cheese, garlic, lemon juice, fish sauce, Worcestershire sauce or anchovy paste, and the remaining salt and pepper, and blend until smooth. If necessary to create a pourable consistency, add milk or buttermilk by the ½ teaspoonful and blend. Place the dressing and chopped lettuce in the bowl with the chicken.

Assemble the wraps. Place the flour tortillas on a flat surface, and divide the dressed chicken and lettuce mixture among the tortillas, placing the mixture on the bottom third of the tortilla. Fold the bottom of the tortilla over the filling, folding away from yourself, then fold the sides in about one-quarter of the way and roll the rest of the tortilla away from yourself tightly to seal. Slice each in half by cross-section and serve immediately.

huevos rancheros wraps

MAKES 6 WRAPS

RANCH-STYLE EGGS, OR HUEVOS RANCHEROS, ARE generally a breakfast dish, but I'm as likely to serve them for lunch, dinner, or as a midafternoon snack. All of the ingredients are basic gluten-free pantry staples, so this is the recipe that you break out when you didn't plan ahead. If you happen to have a ripe avocado on hand, dice the flesh and scatter it on top of the wrap right before serving, with some extra salsa for good measure. These quick wraps are best eaten right away.

2 to 4 tablespoons (28 to 56 g) ghee or clarified butter

6 Soft Tacos (page 205) or 6-inch Corn Tortillas (page 202), warmed in a hot, dry skillet until flexible

8 ounces sharp yellow Cheddar cheese, shredded

6 eggs (300 g, weighed out of shell)

1 cup prepared gluten-free salsa

2 tablespoons chopped fresh cilantro

Place 2 tablespoons ghee in a large cast-iron or nonstick skillet over medium heat. Add one soft taco or corn tortilla and cook until warm and just beginning to brown around the edges, about 1 to 2 minutes. With the tortilla still in the pan, sprinkle one side with 2 tablespoons of shredded cheese. Allow the cheese to melt for about 30 seconds, and then crack one egg into the skillet on top of the melted cheese. Cover the pan and allow the egg to cook for about 3 minutes, until the white begins to set. Top with about 1½ tablespoons of salsa and 2 tablespoons of shredded cheese. Fold the tortilla over on itself, and press down with a wide spatula to adhere and melt the remaining cheese.

Flip the filled tortilla, and cook for another minute or two. Press down on the top firmly to help melt any remaining cheese. Repeat with the remaining tortillas, eggs, and fillings. Serve warm with cilantro.

vegetable spring rolls

MAKES 14 SPRING ROLLS

2 large carrots, julienned

2 scallions, thinly sliced by cross-section

¼ cup fresh bean sprouts

½ cup shredded green cabbage

2 tablespoons (28 g) extra-virgin olive oil

1 tablespoon rice vinegar

2 tablespoons fresh cilantro, chopped

¼ teaspoon kosher salt

⅛ teaspoon freshly ground black pepper

4 ounces dried gluten-free mai fun/rice
    vermicelli noodles (Annie Chun is a
    great brand)

14 8-inch gluten-free rice paper rounds

MAKE-AHEAD OPTION: The vegetables can be sliced and shredded then stored in a sealed container in the refrigerator up to a day ahead of time and can be marinated up to an hour ahead of time. Any longer and they become too wilted and lose their snap. The assembled spring rolls can be stored up to a day in a sealed container separated by plastic wrap or parchment paper in the refrigerator.

SPRING ROLLS ARE REALLY A VERY SPECIAL THING, as quick and easy doesn't even begin to describe them. Both rice paper rounds and mai fun *noodles (thin rice vermicelli noodles) are naturally gluten-free, but you do have to be careful about sourcing them properly. I can't recommend buying them from an Asian food store unless they are certified gluten-free as there is great potential for cross-contamination. But once you find reliable sources for those ingredients, this recipe is a great last-minute dinner choice and perfect as a make-ahead appetizer. The rice paper rounds are surprisingly easy to work with as long as you work quickly and dip them in water only briefly to soften them.*

In a large bowl, place the carrots, scallions, bean sprouts, cabbage, olive oil, vinegar, cilantro, salt, and pepper, and toss to combine well. Allow to sit at room temperature to marinate for about 10 minutes, stirring occasionally. The vegetables will wilt. In a medium bowl, place the dried noodles and cover with boiling water. Allow to soak for 10 minutes, or until the noodles are softened. Drain well, cut into 2-inch pieces with kitchen shears or a sharp knife, and set them aside.

Soften each rice paper round just before filling it. Fill a large bowl with warm water, then dip each round in the water for 5 seconds, or just until softened and translucent. Remove and place on a plate; place about 2 tablespoons of the vegetable mixture and 2 tablespoons of the rice noodles about 1 inch from the lower edge of the rice paper round. Fold the bottom edge of the rice paper securely over the filling, then fold in both sides, roll up tightly, and set aside, seam-side down. Cover the finished rolls with plastic wrap. Refrigerate for 10 minutes (you may also make these ahead of time and refrigerate for several hours). Slice each in half by cross-section and serve chilled.

baked pork spring rolls

LIKE VEGETABLE SPRING ROLLS (PAGE 108), THESE spring rolls can be served unbaked, but the cooked ground pork lends itself to being baked into a crispier wrap. The combination of ground pork, soy sauce, sesame oil, and freshly grated ginger is the key to these spring rolls' special taste, and it mellows beautifully during baking.

Preheat your oven to 400°F. Line a large rimmed baking sheet with unbleached parchment paper, and set it aside.

In a medium-size, heavy-bottomed skillet over medium heat, place the ground pork and the garlic clove. Cook, breaking up the meat, until the meat is browned and the garlic is fragrant, about 5 minutes. Remove the skillet from the heat, discard the garlic, and drain any grease.

In a medium bowl, place the cabbage, carrots, scallions, cilantro, sesame oil, soy sauce, and ginger, and whisk to combine. Add the cooked pork and mix to combine.

Arrange the first wonton wrapper square with a corner facing you. Place about 2 tablespoons of filling about 1 inch from the corner of the wrapper. Fold over the corner and roll one turn away from yourself, making sure to roll as tightly as possible and to prevent any trapped air bubbles. Fold in the sides securely, and continue to roll until the roll is completely sealed. Repeat with the remaining wrappers and filling.

Arrange the spring rolls in a single layer on the prepared baking sheet about 1 inch apart from one another. Brush the outside of the spring rolls lightly with the egg wash. Place in the center of the preheated oven and bake for 10 minutes or until lightly golden brown. Turn the rolls over, brush the other side lightly with egg wash, and return to the oven to continue baking until lightly golden brown all over, about another 6 minutes. Slice each in half by cross-section and serve immediately.

MAKES 10 SPRING ROLLS

½ pound ground pork
1 garlic clove, smashed and peeled
1 cup shredded green cabbage
1 large carrot, cut into a julienne
2 scallions, thinly sliced by cross-section
2 tablespoons chopped fresh cilantro
1 teaspoon toasted sesame oil
2 tablespoons gluten-free soy sauce or tamari
2 teaspoons grated fresh ginger (or 1 teaspoon dried ginger)
1 recipe Wonton Wrappers (page 191), shaped into 10 7-inch squares
Egg wash (1 egg beaten with 1 tablespoon water)

⎯⎯⎯⎯ ☙ ⎯⎯⎯⎯

MAKE-AHEAD OPTION: The vegetables can be sliced and shredded then stored in a sealed container in the refrigerator up to a day ahead of time and can be marinated up to an hour ahead of time. The assembled spring rolls can be stored up to a day in a sealed container separated by plastic wrap or parchment paper in the refrigerator, and then brushed with the egg wash and baked before serving. Once baked, they are best eaten right away.

⎯⎯⎯⎯ ☙ ⎯⎯⎯⎯

spinach lasagna roll-ups

1 28-ounce can tomato purée (or purée one 28-ounce can of whole peeled tomatoes until smooth)

1 tablespoon dried oregano

2 teaspoons dried basil

1 teaspoon garlic powder

½ teaspoon onion powder

1¼ teaspoons kosher salt, divided

1 10-ounce package frozen whole-leaf spinach, thawed

12 gluten-free lasagna noodles, uncooked

2 eggs (100 g, weighed out of shell), beaten

1 pound ricotta cheese

12 ounces part-skim mozzarella cheese, shredded, divided

2 ounces Parmigiano-Reggiano cheese, finely grated

⅛ teaspoon freshly ground black pepper

—————— ✧ ——————

MAKE-AHEAD OPTION: Lasagna roll-ups can be assembled ahead of time, placed in a greased baking dish without the tomato sauce or shredded mozzarella cheese on top, wrapped tightly, and frozen. Defrost overnight in the refrigerator, spoon all of the tomato sauce over the top, top with the shredded cheese, and bake as directed.

—————— ✧ ——————

LASAGNA ROLL-UPS ARE A QUICK AND EASY WAY TO make this cheesy Italian comfort food in single-serving portions, which comes in handy when you're not entirely sure who is going to show up for dinner when. In my house, I try try try to at least have the children all eat at the same time with me, but reality is that sometimes they eat in shifts. I can pull a few of these roll-ups out and bake as many as I need at a time. That way, no one feels like they're eating "leftovers," which one of my ungrateful children reads as "poison." To make miniature roll-ups, try slicing each cooked lasagna noodle in half along the length, filling and rolling tightly, and continuing with the recipe instructions.

Preheat your oven to 350°F. In a large bowl, place the tomato purée, oregano, basil, garlic powder, onion powder, and 1 teaspoon salt, and whisk to combine well. Place about 1 cup of the tomato sauce in a greased 13 x 9-inch baking dish and spread into an even layer. Set the remaining tomato sauce and the baking dish aside.

Place the thawed spinach in a large tea towel, close the towel around the spinach, and wring it out to release as much of the water as possible. Chop the spinach roughly and set it aside.

In a large pot of salted boiling water, cook the lasagna noodles according to package directions to an al dente texture. Drain the hot water, fill the pot with cold water, leave the noodles in the water, and set the pot aside.

In a large bowl, combine the eggs, ricotta cheese, about 8 ounces of the mozzarella cheese, the Parmigiano-Reggiano cheese, chopped spinach, remaining salt, and pepper.

Remove the lasagna noodles from the water one at a time, blot them dry, and place on a flat surface. Spread ⅓ cup cheese mixture on top of each noodle, and carefully roll the noodle from end to end, beginning at a short side. Place the filled lasagna roll-ups in the baking dish on top of the tomato sauce, seam-side down. Cover with the remaining tomato sauce, and top with the remaining 4 ounces of shredded mozzarella cheese.

Place the baking dish in the center of the preheated oven and bake for about 20 minutes or until the cheeses are melted and the sauce is bubbling. Serve immediately.

spinach and ricotta crêpes

CRÊPES MAY LOOK, SOUND, AND EVEN TASTE DELI-cate, but they can actually stand up to a significant amount of handling in the kitchen once they have cooled a bit. So don't be afraid of overstuffing them with this delicious spinach and ricotta filling. The light sprinkling of Gruyère cheese before these crêpes go into the oven adds a distinct nuttiness to an otherwise pleas-antly mild dish. Once they cool, they can be wrapped in plastic or foil and eaten on the go as well as any burrito.

Make the crêpes according to the recipe instructions. Stack the finished crêpes on a plate and cover with plastic wrap to keep moist.

Bring a large pot of salted water to a boil and add the spin-ach. Return the water to a boil, then remove the pot from the heat. Drain the spinach and rinse it under cold water. Place the blanched spinach in a tea towel or nut milk bag and squeeze to remove as much water as possible. Chop the spinach roughly.

In a large skillet, melt 2 tablespoons of the butter over medium-low heat. Add the chopped onions and sauté, stirring frequently, until nearly translucent, about 5 minutes. Add the spinach, salt, pepper, and nutmeg to the pan, and cook, stirring frequently, until the spinach is dry, about 2 minutes. Remove the skillet from the heat and stir in the ricotta. Add more salt or pepper to taste.

Preheat your oven to 350°F. Grease a large casserole dish (or two smaller ones) generously with unsalted butter and set it aside. Place one crêpe on a work surface and place about 1 tablespoon of filling in the center. Fold the crêpe in half, then in half again, enclosing the filling. Place the filled crêpe, folded-side down, in the prepared baking dish, and sprinkle with the grated cheese. Repeat with the remaining crêpes and filling, overlapping the filled crêpes slightly. Place in the preheated oven and bake until lightly golden brown and bubbling, about 15 minutes. Serve immediately.

MAKES 12 CRÊPES

1 recipe Crêpes (page 197)
1½ pounds baby spinach, washed
2 tablespoons (28 g) unsalted butter, plus
    more for greasing
1 small onion, peeled and chopped
¼ teaspoon kosher salt, or to taste
⅛ teaspoon freshly ground black pepper,
    or to taste
⅛ teaspoon freshly grated nutmeg
1 pound ricotta cheese
4 ounces Gruyère cheese, grated

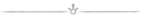

MAKE-AHEAD OPTION: The spinach filling can be made ahead of time and placed in a sealed container in the refrigerator for up to 3 days. If any liquid has leaked out of the filling, simply drain it off before using it. The crêpes themselves can also be made, stacked, covered, and refrigerated for a few hours ahead of time, or stacked, wrapped tightly, and frozen for longer storage. Defrost in the refrigerator, then continue with the recipe as written.

chapter 6: dinner (and lunch, and maybe even breakfast)-to-go

miniature quiches lorraine

QUICHE LORRAINE IS THE ULTIMATE IN SAVORY OPEN-faced custards, filled with smoky bacon and nutty Gruyère cheese. It's such a classic combination, and these miniature quiches are even made more special with a richer crust. If you don't have Gruyère, try substituting with another hard, earthy cheese like Jarlsberg or even Gouda.

Prepare the pastry crust according to the recipe instructions. Preheat your oven to 375°F. Grease 24 miniature brioche molds or two standard 12-cup muffin tins, and set them aside.

On a lightly floured surface, roll out the crust ¼ inch thick, dusting lightly with flour to prevent sticking. Using a 2½-inch round cookie cutter, cut out rounds; gather and reroll scraps and cut out more rounds. Roll out each round until it is slightly more than ⅛ inch thick. Place the rounds in the prepared brioche molds or wells of the prepared muffin tins, pressing gently into the bottom and up the sides. Pierce each crust in the bottom of each pastry with the tines of a fork. Place the pastry crusts in the freezer to chill for 10 minutes.

Remove the chilled crusts from the freezer. Place a small piece of unbleached parchment paper on the bottom of each crust and cover with a few pie weights. Place in the center of the preheated oven and bake until lightly golden brown and matte in appearance, about 8 minutes.

While the crusts are baking, make the filling. Heat a medium-size, heavy-bottomed sauté pan over medium-high heat and add the bacon. Cook, stirring frequently, until the bacon is just starting to brown, about 3 minutes. Remove the cooked bacon from the skillet, leaving behind the rendered fat. Add onion to the pan, and sauté until translucent, about 6 minutes. Add the garlic and cook, stirring frequently, until fragrant, another 2 minutes. Add the bacon back to the skillet, remove from the heat, and set aside to cool briefly. In a large bowl, place the eggs and milk, and whisk to combine well.

Divide the bacon mixture among the blind-baked piecrusts, scatter the cheese on top, and divide the egg mixture among the wells. Place in the oven and bake for 5 minutes. Reduce the heat to 325°F and bake until the filling is set, about another 15 minutes. Allow to sit for 10 minutes before serving.

MAKES 24 QUICHES

FOR THE CRUST

1 recipe Rich Savory Pastry Crust (page 188)

FOR THE FILLING

6 ounces bacon, cut into a large dice
1 small yellow onion, peeled and diced
1 garlic clove, peeled and minced
4 eggs (200 g, weighed out of shell), at room temperature, beaten
1 cup milk (8 fluid ounces), at room temperature
4 ounces Gruyère cheese, grated

MAKE-AHEAD OPTION: The raw crust can be made at least a week ahead of time, wrapped tightly and stored in the refrigerator for at least 5 days (or frozen for longer storage, then defrosted in the refrigerator). The crusts can be blind-baked and stored, unfilled, but they are difficult to wrap without breaking them, so I don't recommend it. The filling is easy enough to make, so I don't recommend making it ahead, either. They are best eaten right away, as baked crust doesn't refrigerate well.

BIGGER BITE OPTION: Make this into a traditional quiche Lorraine by rolling out the pastry crust to fit your standard 9-inch pie plate, piercing the bottom of the pastry, and blind-baking for 10 minutes with pie weights at 375°F. Make the filling as directed and pour into the single, blind-baked pastry crust, and bake in the center of the preheated oven at 350°F until the filling is set, about 50 minutes.

miniature spinach quiches

MAKES 24 QUICHES

FOR THE CRUST

1 recipe Rich Savory Pastry Crust
(page 188)

FOR THE FILLING

8 ounces chopped frozen spinach

2 tablespoons (28 g) extra-virgin olive oil

1 small yellow onion, peeled and diced

4 eggs (200 g, weighed out of shell), at
room temperature, beaten

1 cup (8 fluid ounces) milk, at room
temperature

4 ounces sharp yellow Cheddar cheese,
grated

SPINACH QUICHE IS ANOTHER CLASSIC COMBINA-tion, and one of the only ways two of my three children will eat spinach without complaint. It's not that I don't understand their reluctance. Eaten alone, there's something in spinach that can create a mildly unpleasant mouthfeel that I'm more than willing to power through because of its other many wonderful qualities, but mixed with onion, milk, cheese, and eggs it's a pure delight. As always when baking with spinach, or any other vegetable that contains moisture when cooked, like cauliflower, be very diligent when wringing out all the moisture before baking. Otherwise, the moisture will be released during baking, and your quiche will be watery.

Prepare the pastry crust according to the recipe instructions. Preheat your oven to 375°F. Grease 24 miniature brioche molds or two standard 12-cup muffin tins, and set them aside.

Turn the pastry crust out onto a lightly floured surface and roll out ¼ inch thick, dusting lightly with flour as necessary to prevent sticking. Using a 2½-inch round cookie cutter, cut out rounds; gather and reroll scraps and cut out more rounds. Roll out each round until it is slightly more than ⅛ inch thick, again dusting with more flour as necessary to prevent sticking. Place the rounds in the prepared brioche molds or wells of the prepared muffin tins, pressing gently into the bottom and up the sides. Pierce each crust in the bottom of each pastry with the tines of a fork. Place the pastry crusts in the freezer to chill for 10 minutes or until firm.

Remove the chilled crusts from the freezer. Place a small piece of unbleached parchment paper on the bottom of each crust and cover with a few pie weights. Place the crusts in the center of the preheated oven and bake until lightly golden brown and matte in appearance, about 8 minutes.

While the crusts are baking, make the filling. Defrost the spinach according to the instructions on the package. Place the spinach in a large tea towel or nut milk bag, and twist to wring out as much moisture as possible. Place the oil in a medium-size, heavy-bottomed sauté pan over medium-high heat until it shimmers. Add the onion and cook, stirring frequently, until it's translucent, about 6 minutes. Add the chopped spinach, and stir to combine and break up the spinach. Remove from the heat and set aside to cool briefly.

In a large bowl, place the eggs and milk, and whisk to combine well.

Divide the spinach mixture among the blind-baked piecrusts, scatter the cheese on top evenly, and divide the egg mixture among the wells. Place the quiches in the oven and bake for 5 minutes before reducing the heat to 325°F and baking until the filling is set, about another 15 minutes. Allow the quiches to sit for 10 minutes before serving.

MAKE-AHEAD OPTION: The raw crust can be made at least a week ahead of time, wrapped tightly and stored in the refrigerator for at least 5 days (or frozen for longer storage, then defrosted in the refrigerator). The crusts can be blind-baked and stored, unfilled, but they are difficult to wrap without breaking them, so I don't recommend it. The filling is easy enough to make, so I don't recommend making it ahead, either. They are best eaten right away after baking, as baked crust doesn't refrigerate well.

BIGGER BITE OPTION: Make this into a traditional quiche by rolling out the pastry crust to fit your standard 9-inch pie plate, piercing the bottom of the pastry, and blind-baking for 10 minutes with pie weights at 375°F. Make the filling as directed and pour into the single, blind-baked pastry crust and bake in the center of the preheated oven at 350°F until the filling is set, about 50 minutes.

beef stromboli

LIKE A CROSS BETWEEN A STUFFED PIZZA AND A crispy browned sandwich, this flavorful stromboli is the perfect way to feed that hungry crowd that came over to watch the game, or just your family when they're eating on the run. If your family doesn't love beef, substitute cooked gluten-free sausage or even shredded cooked chicken. But don't hold back on the spices, or the cheese!

MAKES 24 PORTIONS

1 recipe Thin Crust Pizza Dough
  (page 214)
1 pound 90% lean ground beef
2 eggs (100 g, weighed out of shell), lightly
  beaten
3 tablespoons (42 g) extra-virgin olive oil
½ teaspoon garlic powder
½ teaspoon onion powder
1 teaspoon dried basil
½ teaspoon dried oregano
½ teaspoon kosher salt
12 ounces part-skim mozzarella cheese,
  shredded
1 small onion, peeled and diced

MAKE-AHEAD OPTION: The ground beef can be cooked ahead of time, then cooled and stored in a sealed container in the refrigerator for up to 3 days before using. Once fully prepared, this stromboli is best eaten right away.

Make the pizza dough according to the recipe instructions and place the dough in a sealed container or bowl in a warm, draft-free location to rise until nearly doubled in size (1 to 2 hours, depending upon environment). Full doubling is not necessary. Place the risen dough, still in a sealed container or bowl, in the refrigerator to chill until firmer, about 30 minutes. Alternatively, set the dough to rise in a sealed container in the refrigerator for about 12 hours or up to 5 days.

On baking day, preheat your oven to 375°F. Line a large rimmed baking sheet with unbleached parchment paper, and set it aside. In a medium-size, heavy-bottomed skillet, cook the ground beef over medium-high heat, stirring occasionally, until no pink remains. Drain any fat from the meat, and set it aside. Divide the dough in half and turn out one-half onto a lightly floured surface, keeping the other half covered lightly with a tea towel. Sprinkle lightly with extra flour and fold and turn the dough until it is a bit smoother, sprinkling again lightly with more flour to prevent the dough from sticking. Place the prepared piece of dough on a large, lightly oiled piece of unbleached piece of parchment paper, and shape into a 12 x 10-inch rectangle, shifting the dough frequently and sprinkling lightly with extra flour to prevent sticking or tearing.

In a small bowl, place the beaten eggs, oil, garlic powder, onion powder, basil, oregano, and salt, and whisk to combine well. Using a pastry brush, brush the egg mixture all over the dough, leaving a ½-inch border all around the edge. Layer about half of the cooked beef, shredded cheese, and diced onion on the dough to within ½ inch of the edges. Press the fillings down lightly to help them adhere to the dough. Beginning with a long side, roll the dough up and over the fillings, using the oiled parchment paper to coax the dough to create a coil. End with the roll seam-side up. Invert the roll, so it is

seam-side down, onto the prepared baking sheet. Repeat with the remaining half of the dough and the remaining fillings. Place the stromboli about 2 inches apart and brush the tops with the remaining egg mixture.

Place the baking sheet in the center of the preheated oven and bake for 25 to 30 minutes or until lightly golden brown all over. Remove from the oven and allow to sit for about 5 minutes before slicing each by cross-section into 12 pieces and serving warm.

chicken empanadas

THERE IS JUST NO LIMIT TO THE MOUTHWATERING
fillings you might find inside the buttery pastry shell of an
empanada. Chorizo and cheese, or chicken, chiles, and cheese,
or a savory beef and cheese filling (page 125), and pretty much
anything else you can dream up, including even sweet fillings.
One of my favorite combinations is (you guessed it!) chicken,
chiles, and cheese. Increase the flavor and spice by adding more
cumin and chili powder to taste, and swap out the cheeses for
other semihard cheeses if you have another favorite.

Prepare the empanada dough according to the recipe instructions, and cut out 4-inch circles, gathering and rerolling scraps. Sprinkle the empanada rounds lightly with extra flour, then stack them and place them in the refrigerator to chill while you prepare the filling.

Preheat your oven to 375°F. Grease a small, square baking dish with cooking oil spray and place the chicken breast in the center, skin-side up. Sprinkle with the salt and pepper, and drizzle with the olive oil. Place the pan in the center of the preheated oven and bake for 30 minutes, or until the chicken is cooked through and the center registers 165°F on an instant-read thermometer. Remove the chicken from the oven and allow it to cool briefly before separating the flesh from the skin and bones and shredding it with two forks. In a large bowl, place the chopped green chiles, minced garlic, chili powder, cumin, and cinnamon, and mix to combine well. Add the shredded chicken, grated cheeses, and cilantro, and mix until just combined.

Remove the empanada dough from the refrigerator, and place 2 teaspoonsful of filling in the center of each round, then moisten the edges of the dough with wet fingers. Fold the round over the filling, gently pressing out any air, and pinch the edge to seal.

Place paper towels on a plate, and set it aside. Heat 1 inch frying oil in a large skillet until rippling and fry empanadas in a single layer, taking care not to crowd the pan, for about 2 minutes. Flip the empanadas over and continue frying for about 1 minute longer, or until golden brown all over. Remove from the skillet with a slotted spoon and transfer to the paper-towel-lined plate to drain. Repeat with the remaining empanadas. Serve warm.

MAKES ABOUT 25 EMPANADAS

1 recipe Empanada Dough (page 189)
1 pound skin-on, bone-in chicken breast
¾ teaspoon kosher salt
⅛ teaspoon freshly ground black pepper
1 tablespoon (14 g) extra-virgin olive oil
1 4-ounce can chopped green chiles
2 garlic cloves, peeled and minced
½ teaspoon ground chipotle chili powder
1 teaspoon ground cumin
¼ teaspoon ground cinnamon
2 ounces Monterey Jack cheese, grated
2 ounces yellow Cheddar cheese, grated
2 tablespoons chopped fresh cilantro, plus more for serving
Neutral oil, for frying

MAKE-AHEAD OPTION: The empanadas can be shaped and filled, then placed, raw, in a single layer on a baking sheet and frozen. Pile them into a freezer-safe bag and return them to the freezer. Defrost overnight in the refrigerator and pat dry before frying.

NO-FRY OPTION: Follow the recipe instructions as written for shaping and filling the empanadas, but line a large rimmed baking sheet with unbleached parchment paper. Place the raw empanadas on the prepared baking sheet about 1 inch apart. Using a pastry brush, coat the tops with an egg wash (1 egg beaten with 1 tablespoon water), then bake for 10 minutes at 375°F. Turn the empanadas over and bake for 5 minutes more, or until lightly golden brown.

BIGGER BITE OPTION: Shape the rounds of empanada dough to 6 inches in diameter, double the filling, and proceed with the recipe as written. For frying, increase the frying time by about another 2 minutes total. For baking, increase the baking time to about 20 minutes total.

beef empanadas

ALONG WITH CHICKEN, CHILES, AND CHEESE (PAGE 123), beef empanadas are one of my favorites. I love this classic Argentine combination of beef, hard boiled egg, olives, and raisins, which has all the flavors (savory and lightly sweet!) and textures (firm, soft, and flaky!) you could ever want.

Prepare the empanada dough according to the recipe instructions, and cut out 4-inch circles, gathering and rerolling scraps. Sprinkle the empanada rounds lightly with extra flour, then stack them and place them in the refrigerator to chill while you prepare the filling.

In a 12-inch skillet, heat the ghee or clarified butter over medium heat. Add the onion and sauté on medium, stirring frequently, until it begins to soften, about 4 minutes. Add the ground beef, and cook until the beef is lightly browned and the onion is translucent and soft, about 5 minutes. Add the salt, pepper, cumin, paprika, and chili powder, and mix to combine. Remove the skillet from the heat, drain any liquid, and set the filling aside to cool briefly.

Place 1 teaspoonful of the beef filling in the center of each round, top with a slice of hard boiled egg, a couple olive slices, and a couple raisins. Moisten the edges of the dough with wet fingers, fold the round over the filling, gently pressing out any air, and pinch the edge to seal.

Place paper towels on a plate, and set it aside. Heat 1 inch frying oil in a large skillet until rippling and fry empanadas in a single layer, taking care not to crowd the pan, for about 1 minute per side or until golden brown. Remove from the skillet with a slotted spoon and transfer to the paper-towel-lined dish to drain. Repeat with the remaining empanadas.

MAKES ABOUT 25 EMPANADAS

1 recipe Empanada Dough (page 189)
2 tablespoons (28 g) ghee or clarified butter
1 small yellow onion, peeled and finely chopped
½ pound 90% lean ground beef
¾ teaspoon kosher salt
⅛ teaspoon freshly ground black pepper
½ teaspoon ground cumin
½ teaspoon smoked paprika
⅛ teaspoon chili powder
2 hard boiled eggs, sliced
3 ounces cured black olives, pitted and sliced
¼ cup raisins
Neutral oil, for shallow frying

———————— ⚜ ————————

MAKE-AHEAD OPTION: The empanadas can be shaped and filled, then placed, raw, in a single layer on a baking sheet and frozen. Pile them into a freezer-safe bag and return them to the freezer. Defrost overnight in the refrigerator and pat dry before frying.

NO-FRY OPTION: Follow the recipe instructions as written for shaping and filling the empanadas, but line a large rimmed baking sheet with unbleached parchment paper. Place the raw empanadas on the prepared baking sheet about 1 inch apart. Using a pastry brush, coat the tops with an egg wash (1 egg beaten with 1 tablespoon water), then bake for 10 minutes at 375°F. Turn the empanadas over and bake for 5 minutes more, or until lightly golden brown.

BIGGER BITE OPTION: Shape the rounds of empanada dough to 6 inches in diameter, double the filling, and proceed with the recipe as written. For frying, increase the frying time by about another 2 minutes total. For baking, increase the baking time to about 20 minutes total.

———————— ⚜ ————————

vegetable and cheese quesadillas

MAKES 4 SERVINGS

3 tablespoons (42 g) extra-virgin olive oil, plus more for brushing

3 garlic cloves, smashed and peeled

1 small yellow onion, peeled and diced

1 pound fresh zucchini, thinly sliced in cross-section

4 ounces frozen corn kernels

8 8-inch Flour Tortillas (page 198)

4 ounces Monterey Jack cheese, shredded

4 ounces sharp yellow Cheddar cheese, shredded

———————— ✂ ————————

MAKE-AHEAD OPTION: The vegetables can be sautéed ahead of time, cooled to room temperature, then stored in a sealed container in the refrigerator for up to 3 days. Before using, allow them to come to room temperature. Once fully prepared, the quesadillas are best eaten right away.

———————— ✂ ————————

THE ONLY TIME THAT I WOULD EVEN CONSIDER SUGgesting you use packaged gluten-free flour tortillas is in a quesadilla. You don't need the tortilla to bend like you do in a burrito (page 137), and you're melting cheese all over them. Of course, the fresh kind are so much better, and the delicious combination of savory sautéed onion and zucchini with sweet corn certainly doesn't hurt. Try adding sautéed mushrooms in place of (or along with) the zucchini for a meatier taste.

In a medium-size sauté pan with a cover, heat the olive oil over medium heat and add the smashed garlic cloves. Cook, turning once, until the oil is fragrant and the garlic is browned, about 2 minutes. Discard the garlic. Add the onion to the oil and cook, stirring occasionally, until translucent, about 6 minutes. Add the zucchini, cover and cook until the zucchini is tender, stirring occasionally to ensure that the zucchini does not stick to the bottom of the pan, about 8 minutes. Remove the cover, add the frozen corn, and stir until the corn is defrosted. Remove the pan from the heat.

Heat a 12-inch cast-iron skillet (or nonstick omelet pan) over medium heat. Brush one side of each of the 8 tortillas lightly with olive oil and place one tortilla, oiled-side down, in the hot skillet. Place about one-quarter of the zucchini-corn mixture on top of the tortilla in an even layer, and top with about 1 ounce of each of the grated cheeses in an even layer. Place another tortilla, oiled-side up, on top. Press down firmly on the top tortilla and cook until the bottom tortilla is beginning to crisp. Flip the quesadilla, and continue to cook until the other side of the quesadilla is browned and crisp. Remove the quesadilla from the pan and slice into wedges. Repeat with the other tortillas and remaining vegetables and cheese. Serve immediately.

vegetarian chalupas

YOU CAN BUY CRUNCHY CORN CHALUPA SHELLS ready-made (Charras brand is even gluten-free in the United States), but making your own from fresh corn tortillas is very simple and, of course, tastes much more authentic (page 202). As always, if you'd like to kick up the heat, use spicier canned green chiles, and add ground chipotle chili powder to the tomato mixture. This recipe calls for cotija cheese, a hard Mexican cheese with a very mild flavor. Feta cheese is saltier, but is of similar consistency, so would be a good substitute.

In a large, heavy-bottomed saucepan, heat the oil over medium heat and sauté the diced onion, stirring frequently, until translucent, about 6 minutes. Add the chopped green chiles and diced tomatoes, bring to a simmer, and allow to cook, uncovered, for about 8 minutes, or until the mixture begins to thicken. Remove the saucepan from the heat and set it aside.

Place the tortillas on a large parchment-lined baking sheet and spray on both sides with cooking oil spray. Preheat your oven's broiler, and place the tortillas about 5 inches under the broiler until golden brown on one side (less than 2 minutes). Remove from the oven, flip the tortillas over, and place them back under the broiler until golden brown on the other side (less than 2 minutes more). Remove from the oven and allow to cool briefly.

To serve, spread a thick layer of refried beans on each tortilla, then top with the tomato and chile mixture, then the Monterey jack cheese, cotija crumbles, and scallions. Serve warm, with sour cream.

MAKES 10 CHALUPAS

2 tablespoons (28 g) extra-virgin olive oil
1 small onion, peeled and diced
1 4-ounce can chopped mild green chiles
1 14-ounce can diced tomatoes
10 8-inch Corn Tortillas (page 202)
1 15-ounce can vegetarian refried beans
4 ounces Monterey jack cheese, shredded
4 ounces cotija cheese (or feta), crumbled
2 scallions, chopped
Sour cream, for serving

———————⚜———————

MAKE-AHEAD OPTION: The tomato, chiles, and onion mixture can be made ahead of time and stored in a sealed container in the refrigerator for up to 3 days. Allow to come to room temperature before proceeding with the recipe. Once fully prepared, the chalupas are best eaten right away.

———————⚜———————

pupusas

MAKES 6 PUPUSAS

2 cups (232 g) gluten-free masa harina corn flour

½ teaspoon kosher salt

1½ cups (12 fluid ounces) warm water

1 15-ounce can black beans, drained and rinsed

1 teaspoon ground cumin

¼ teaspoon chili powder

10 ounces Monterey Jack cheese, grated

PUPUSAS *ARE LIKE STUFFED FRESH CORN TORTILLAS, as the shell is made of masa harina, salt, and water, just like Corn Tortillas (page 202). Instead of being rolled flat, the simple, fragrant dough is wrapped around the filling. Here, the filling is as simple as can be, but still deeply flavorful and comforting: spiced beans and cheese. As long as you resist the urge to overstuff the pupusas, you can add cooked ground beef or cooked shredded chicken, or replace the seasoned black beans with refried beans. Let your tastes be your guide.*

Line a rimmed baking sheet with parchment paper, and set it aside. In a large bowl, place the masa harina and salt and whisk to combine. Create a well in the center of the dry ingredients, add about 10 ounces of the water, and mix until a thick dough forms. The dough should be a bit tacky to the touch but not too soft and not crumbly. Add more water by the tablespoonful and mix to combine to achieve the right consistency. Cover the bowl and set it aside for 5 minutes to allow the masa to absorb the liquid.

While the dough is resting, in a separate, medium-size bowl, place the beans. Add the ground cumin and chili powder, and mix to combine. Place the cheese in a small bowl beside the beans. Place a small bowl with warm water, also beside the cheese.

Check the dough. If it appears too dry, add a tablespoon of water; wet your hands in the water bowl, and work the water in to the dough. Once the dough is ready, divide it into 6 equal parts. Roll each piece of dough into a ball with wet hands. Then, in a rhythmic motion, pat the dough between wet palms until it flattens. If it splits along the edges, just press it back together. A tight seal around the edges is not necessary as they will not rise during cooking.

Press the center of the flattened dough gently into the palm of your hand to create a well for the filling. Add a couple of tablespoons of grated cheese to the center, then top with about one-sixth of the bean mixture. The dough will be nearly covered with filling. Then, with the hand that is cradling the *pupusa,* begin to close the edges of the dough toward the center, rotating the ball in your hand as you work. Your free hand should help to thin the dough a bit to cover the filling. Once the filling

MAKE-AHEAD OPTION: These can be made and cooked ahead of time, then wrapped individually with freezer-safe wrap and frozen for up to 2 months. Defrost at room temperature and reheat in the microwave or, after blotting dry, in a hot, dry skillet for about 30 seconds on each side.

is covered with the dough, pat the dough flat again between moistened palms and place the shaped *pupusa* on the prepared baking sheet. Repeat with the remaining dough and filling. Cover the shaped *pupusas* lightly with a tea towel so they don't dry out.

Heat a cast-iron pan or other griddle over medium-high heat. If using a nonstick pan, do not place over anything other than medium heat. Place the *pupusas* on the hot pan in batches, taking care not to crowd the pan, and cook until firm, about 3 or 4 minutes per side. Repeat with the remaining shaped *pupusas*. Serve warm.

chicken gorditas

THE CORN CAKES FOR GORDITAS ARE DIFFERENT than Pupusas (page 130) in a few important ways. In addition to masa harina and water, they're made with a small amount of all-purpose gluten-free flour, plus baking powder and some shortening, all of which helps them in their second difference. Their second difference is that they're considerably lighter and fluffier than pupusas—and they're sliced in half and served with filling, like a sandwich. I enjoy these deeply satisfying corn cakes so much that I make double (and triple!) batches of them and stock my freezer. Sometimes I serve them with this garlicky tomato chicken filling, and sometimes just a sliced tomato and a fried egg. Heaven!

Cook the chicken. Place the chicken breasts on a greased and lined baking sheet, sprinkle them on both sides with salt and pepper, and drizzle them with olive oil. Place them under your oven's broiler for about 12 minutes, flipping them about halfway through, or until they are cooked all the way through and reach 165°F on an instant-read thermometer. Allow the chicken to cool briefly before cutting it into a large dice and setting it aside.

Make the filling. Place all of the filling ingredients except for the cooked chicken in a medium-size, heavy-bottomed saucepan. Bring to a simmer over medium heat and cook, stirring occasionally, until the mixture begins to thicken, about 10 minutes. Add the cooked chicken to the pan, remove it from the heat, and set the filling aside.

Make the corn cakes. In a large bowl, place the masa harina, flour, baking powder, and salt, and whisk to combine well. Create a well in the center of the dry ingredients, add the melted shortening and about 1¾ cups (14 fluid ounces) of the water, and mix until a thick dough forms. The dough should be a bit tacky to the touch but not too soft and not crumbly. Add more water by the tablespoonful and mix to combine to achieve the right consistency. Cover the bowl and set it aside for 5 minutes to allow the masa to absorb the liquid.

Divide the dough into 8 pieces (about 4½ ounces each) and, with wet hands, pat each into a circle about 4 inches in diameter and about ½ inch thick. If the edges crack, moisten your fingers and smooth them out. Heat a cast-iron pan or other griddle over medium-high heat. If using a nonstick pan, do not place over

FOR THE FILLING

1½ pounds skinless, boneless chicken breasts

1 teaspoon kosher salt

⅛ teaspoon freshly ground black pepper

2 tablespoons (28 g) extra virgin olive oil

¼ cup (2 fluid ounces) chicken stock

1 14-ounce can fire-roasted diced tomatoes

1 medium red onion, peeled and minced

1 garlic clove, smashed and peeled

2 tablespoons fresh chopped cilantro

1 teaspoon ground cumin

½ teaspoon ground chili powder

FOR THE CORN CAKES

3½ cups (406 g) gluten-free masa harina corn flour

½ cup (70 g) all-purpose gluten-free flour (page 2)

2 teaspoons baking powder

¾ teaspoon kosher salt

4 tablespoons (48 g) nonhydrogenated vegetable shortening, melted and cooled

2¼ cups (18 fluid ounces) warm water

Neutral oil, for frying

FOR SERVING

Chopped iceberg lettuce

Diced fresh tomatoes

Shredded pepper Jack cheese

anything other than medium heat. Place the corn cakes on the hot pan in batches, taking care not to crowd the pan, and cook until lightly golden brown and firm to the touch, about 3 to 4 minutes per side.

Place paper towels on a plate, and set it aside. Place 1 inch of oil in a medium-size, heavy-bottomed pot over medium-high heat until the oil ripples. Place the gorditas in the hot oil in batches and fry, turning once, until golden brown all over, about 3 minutes total. Remove from the hot oil and allow to drain on the paper-towel-lined plate. Repeat with the remaining corn cakes. Using a large serrated knife, slice in half horizontally. Fill with the chicken and salsa mixture, plus shredded lettuce, diced tomatoes, and shredded cheese.

MAKE-AHEAD OPTION: The corn cakes can be made and cooked in a dry pan, but not fried, then cooled completely, wrapped tightly, and frozen for up to 2 months. Defrost at room temperature, pat dry, and then fry before serving. The filling can be made ahead of time and stored in a sealed container in the refrigerator for up to 3 days, then warmed gently over low heat in a saucepan before serving.

soft beef tacos

MAKES 8 TACOS

FOR THE FILLING

1 tablespoon chili powder

2 tablespoons ground cumin

2 tablespoons smoked Spanish paprika

1 teaspoon ground coriander

1 tablespoon (9 g) Basic Gum-Free Gluten-
Free Flour (page 4)

1½ teaspoons kosher salt

2 tablespoons (28 g) extra-virgin olive oil

1 large red onion, peeled and diced

4 garlic cloves, smashed and peeled

1½ pounds 90% lean ground beef

½ cup (4 fluid ounces) lukewarm water

FOR SERVING

8 Soft Tacos (page 205) or Corn Tortillas
(page 202)

2 ounces sharp yellow Cheddar cheese,
shredded

2 ounces Monterey Jack cheese, shredded

MAKE-AHEAD OPTION: The filling can be
made ahead of time and stored in a sealed
container in the refrigerator for up to
3 days. It is best to warm it through before
using it to make the tacos, which can be
done in a microwave at 60% power or in a
warm skillet. If the filling seems to be at all
dry, mix a couple of tablespoons of water
into the filling and in the skillet. Proceed
with the recipe as directed.

WE'VE NEVER REALLY ADOPTED THE WHOLE TACO
Tuesdays thing at my house, but whenever I make tacos and find
that it's to everyone's delight, I wonder why not. These spicy soft
beef tacos are assembled in the pan, which allows the cheese to
melt nicely into the beef mixture. Once cooled, simply wrap the
tacos loosely in foil and they're easily portable. If your schedule
allows you to sit down and eat, serve the warmed tortillas, beef
filling, and shredded cheese without assembling the tacos, and
allow your dinner companions to build their own.

In a small bowl, place the chili powder, ground cumin, paprika,
coriander, flour, and salt, and whisk to combine well. Set aside.
Place the olive oil in a large, heavy-bottomed skillet over
medium heat, then add the onion and garlic. Cook until the
onion is beginning to soften and the garlic is fragrant, about
4 minutes. Remove and discard the garlic. Add the ground beef
to the skillet and cook until it's no longer pink, breaking up the
beef and turning it occasionally as it cooks. Add the chili powder mixture and the water, stir to combine and simmer, uncovered, until the mixture has begun to thicken, about 5 minutes.

Heat a 9-inch cast-iron or nonstick skillet over medium heat.
Place the soft tacos, one at a time, in the skillet until softened,
about 1 minute. With the taco still in the skillet, sprinkle about
1 tablespoon of each type of shredded cheese evenly on top,
then ¼ cup of the ground beef filling on one-half of the taco.
Using tongs, fold the taco over and press to help the cheese
adhere. Repeat with the remaining soft tacos, cheese, and filling.
Serve warm.

crispy black bean burritos

THERE ARE A FEW HANDHELD DINNER (OR LUNCH) meals that I endeavor to always have on hand, in case of "emergencies," in other words, what my children call it when they're hungry and I didn't plan ahead. Crispy Black Bean Burritos are one of them. Once the Flour Tortillas (page 198) are made (another staple I keep on hand in my freezer always), these take mere minutes to assemble and as an added bonus are hearty and satisfying any day of the week. You can of course modify the spices to suit your and your family's personal tastes, but the concept is sound and can feel like a real lifesaver when the dinner hour is nearly upon you.

Place the olive oil in a large, heavy-bottomed skillet over medium heat, add the onion and garlic, and sauté, stirring frequently, until the onion is beginning to soften and the garlic is fragrant, about 4 minutes. Remove and discard the garlic. Add the salt, pepper, cumin, chili powder, lime juice, black beans, and frozen corn, and mix to combine. Allow to cook until much of the liquid has evaporated, about 3 minutes. Remove the pan from the heat and set it aside.

Heat a 9-inch cast-iron or stainless steel skillet over medium heat and warm the tortillas, one at a time, until softened. To assemble each burrito, lay one tortilla on a flat surface, and on the lower third of the tortilla, place about ¼ cup of the black bean mixture, 2 tablespoons rice, and about ¼ cup of cheese, leaving a clean 1-inch border along the bottom edge of the tortilla. Fold the bottom of the tortilla up over the filling, fold in the sides over the bottom fold, and then roll away from yourself to tightly to seal. Repeat with the remaining tortillas and fillings.

Place 1 tablespoon of ghee or clarified butter in the skillet and melt over medium heat. Place each of the formed burritos in the hot skillet, seam-side down, and cook for about 1 minute per side or until lightly golden brown and crispy, and serve warm.

MAKES 8 BURRITOS

FOR THE FILLING

2 tablespoons (28 g) extra-virgin olive oil
1 small red onion, peeled and finely chopped
1 garlic clove, smashed and peeled
1 teaspoon kosher salt
⅛ teaspoon freshly ground black pepper
1 teaspoon ground cumin
⅛ teaspoon chili powder
2 tablespoons freshly squeezed lime juice
1 15-ounce can black beans, drained and rinsed
5 ounces frozen corn

FOR SERVING

8 8-inch Flour Tortillas (page 198)
1 cup cooked brown rice
4 ounces Monterey Jack cheese, shredded
2 to 3 tablespoons (28 to 42 g) ghee or clarified butter

MAKE-AHEAD OPTION: Burritos freeze amazingly well. Assemble the burritos entirely, and wrap each tightly in freezer-safe wrap individually after they are filled and formed, but before they are browned in the skillet, and freeze for up to 2 months. Defrost in the refrigerator overnight or at room temperature, pat dry, and then brown in the skillet as directed.

chicken gyros

I'M BREAKING ALL THE RULES WITH THESE CHICKEN gyros. Tzatziki is technically not meant to be made with fresh dill (but it's so delicious!), gyros are meant to be served on (or in) pita bread, and the meat is traditionally cooked on a rotisserie. Once you taste the tenderness of the skinless, boneless chicken after it's been marinated in a garlic-lemon-yogurt sauce, try my tzatziki with dill, and try a gyro made with tangy naan bread or cheesy soft tapioca wraps, you'll forgive me all of my trespasses. Wrap these tightly in soft tapioca wraps, and slice into pinwheels by cross-section for a small bite suitable to serve as an appetizer.

MAKES 6 GYROS

FOR THE WRAPS

1 recipe Soft Tapioca Cheese Wraps
(page 207) or Naan Bread dough
(page 210), warmed until flexible

FOR THE CHICKEN

2 garlic cloves, peeled and minced
¼ cup freshly squeezed lemon juice
2 tablespoons white wine vinegar
¼ cup (56 g) extra-virgin olive oil
3 tablespoons (43 g) plain yogurt
½ teaspoon kosher salt
⅛ teaspoon freshly ground black pepper
2 pounds skinless, boneless chicken breasts

FOR THE TZATZIKI

½ cup peeled, seeded, and shredded
cucumber
3 garlic cloves, peeled and minced
1 tablespoon white wine vinegar
8 ounces Greek-style plain yogurt
1 tablespoon (14 g) extra-virgin olive oil
1 tablespoon chopped fresh dill, plus more
for sprinkling (optional)
1 tablespoon freshly squeezed lemon juice

FOR SERVING

Tomatoes, seeded and chopped
Red onion, peeled and sliced thinly
Feta cheese, crumbled

MAKE-AHEAD OPTION: The *tzatziki* and the chicken can be made ahead of time and stored in a sealed container in the refrigerator for 3 days. Warm the chicken gently in a saucepan over low heat before serving. If you're using it, the naan dough can be made up to one day ahead of time and stored in a sealed proofing bucket in the refrigerator before shaping and cooking.

First, make the naan or the soft tapioca wraps according to the recipe instructions. Place the wraps or naan in a stack and cover with a tea towel to keep warm.

Marinate the chicken. In a large bowl or zip-top plastic bag, place all of the ingredients for the chicken except for the chicken itself and mix to combine well either with a whisk, or by closing the plastic bag securely and massaging the mixture from outside the bag. Place the chicken breasts in the marinade, and either cover the bowl tightly or close the bag securely. Place in the refrigerator and marinate for 1 hour or for up to 2 days.

Make the *tzatziki*. Place the shredded cucumber in a clean tea towel or nut milk bag, enclose the cucumber tightly, and squeeze tightly to remove as much moisture as possible. Place the cucumber in a medium-size bowl, add the remaining *tzatziki* ingredients, and whisk to combine well. Sprinkle the top with a bit more chopped fresh dill, cover the bowl tightly, and refrigerate until ready to serve.

Cook the chicken. Line a rimmed baking sheet with aluminum foil and grease with cooking spray. Remove the chicken breasts from the marinade, and place side by side on the sheet. Discard any remaining marinade. Place the chicken directly under your oven's broiler and cook for 6 minutes. Remove the chicken from the oven and flip each breast over carefully. Return to the oven and broil until cooked through (4 to 6 minutes more, depending upon the thickness of the chicken breasts). Remove the chicken from the oven, and allow to rest for at least 5 minutes before slicing each breast into strips.

To make each individual gyro, pile strips of chicken, *tzatziki* sauce, tomatoes, red onion, and crumbled feta cheese in the center of a warm tapioca wrap or piece of naan. Fold and serve.

shrimp pot stickers

THERE ARE MANY WAYS TO COOK POT STICKERS, from steaming to sautéing and frying. My favorite way is to sauté them in a hot pan, then add water and cover the pan and allow steam to cook them the rest of the way. Next, you uncover the pan and cook until the water evaporates and the pot stickers are crisp-tender. Cooked this way, the gingery pork and shrimp filling cooks completely without overcooking, the wonton skin stays tender, and the underside of the pot stickers gets golden brown and delicious.

Prepare the wonton wrappers according to the recipe instructions, shaping the wrappers into circles about 3 inches in diameter.

To make the filling, in a medium-size bowl, place the shrimp, pork, cabbage, scallions, ginger, sesame oil, and soy sauce, and mix gently to combine. Place about 1 tablespoon of the shrimp and pork filling in the center of each wrapper. Using a pastry brush, brush the edges of the wrapper lightly with the egg wash, and fold the wrapper over on itself to cover the filling. Pinch the edges to seal the dumpling closed, gently pressing out any trapped air as you go.

In a large, heavy-bottomed skillet over medium-high heat, heat about 2 tablespoons of the neutral oil until rippling. Place the dumplings in a single layer in the hot oil, and sauté until the pot stickers are golden and crisp on the underside, about 1 minute. Add about ¼ cup of lukewarm water to the pan, or enough so that it rises about one-quarter of the way up the sides of the pot stickers. Cover the skillet and steam until the dumplings are cooked through, about 6 minutes. Uncover the skillet and continue to cook until the water has evaporated and the dumplings are crisp-tender, another 2 minutes. Remove from the pan and repeat with the remaining pot stickers. Serve immediately, with more soy sauce for dipping.

MAKES ABOUT 36 POT STICKERS

1 recipe Wonton Wrappers (page 191)
1 pound raw shrimp, peeled, deveined, and diced
½ pound lean ground pork
1 cup finely shredded green cabbage
2 scallions, thinly sliced
1 tablespoon freshly grated ginger (or 1½ teaspoons dried)
1 teaspoon sesame oil
2 tablespoons gluten-free soy sauce or tamari, plus more for serving
Egg wash (1 egg beaten with 1 tablespoon water)
2 to 6 tablespoons (28 to 84 g) neutral oil, for sautéing
Lukewarm water, for cooking

MAKE-AHEAD OPTION: The pot stickers can be shaped and filled, then placed in a single layer on a baking sheet and frozen. Pile them into a freezer-safe bag and return them to the freezer. Defrost overnight in the refrigerator, and pat dry before sautéing. Once sautéed, they are best eaten right away.

handheld chicken potpies

ALL THE TASTE OF CHICKEN POTPIE—IN A WEE LITTLE pocket. These warm, creamy potpies (also called pasties) cook quickly by using shredded carrots and finely chopped celery (to be honest, I believe I could live on the filling alone). If you're looking to make quicker work of these little masterpieces, try shredding the meat of a gluten-free rotisserie chicken and using that in place of the chicken breasts. If you think the buttery, flaky crust of a potpie is the very best part, you'll fall head over heels for this ultraportable version.

Cook the chicken. Place the chicken breasts on a greased and lined baking sheet, sprinkle them on both sides with salt and pepper, and drizzle them with olive oil. Place them under your oven's broiler for about 12 minutes, flipping them about halfway through, or until they are cooked all the way through and reach 165°F on an instant-read thermometer. Allow the chicken to cool briefly before cutting it into a large dice and setting it aside.

Preheat your oven to 375°F. Line rimmed baking sheets with unbleached parchment paper, and set them aside.

Prepare the filling. In a medium-size, heavy-bottomed saucepan, heat the olive oil over medium-high heat. Add the onion, celery, and carrot, and cook until the onions and celery are translucent, about 6 minutes. Transfer to a small bowl, and set it aside. To the same medium-size saucepan, add the butter and melt over medium heat. Add the flour, salt, and pepper, and stir to combine well. The mixture will clump at first, and then smooth. This is the roux that will thicken the sauce. Cook over medium heat, stirring constantly, until the mixture has just begun to turn a very light-brown color, about 2 minutes. Add the stock to the roux very slowly, stirring constantly to break up any lumps that might form. Add the evaporated milk and the thyme, and continue to stir until the mixture is smooth. Bring the mixture to a simmer, and continue to cook, stirring occasionally, until reduced by about one-quarter. Remove the saucepan from the heat, and add the cooked onion mixture. Stir to combine.

MAKES 24 POTPIES

FOR THE CHICKEN

1½ pounds skinless, boneless chicken breasts
1 teaspoon kosher salt
⅛ teaspoon freshly ground black pepper
2 tablespoons (28 g) extra-virgin olive oil

FOR THE FILLING

2 tablespoons (28 g) extra-virgin olive oil
1 small onion, peeled and finely chopped
1 stalk celery, finely chopped
1 large carrot, peeled and shredded
2 tablespoons (28 g) unsalted butter
3 tablespoons (27 g) Basic Gum-Free Gluten-Free Flour (page 4)
½ teaspoon kosher salt
⅛ teaspoon freshly ground black pepper
1 cup (8 fluid ounces) chicken stock
8 fluid ounces low-fat evaporated milk
1 tablespoon fresh thyme (or 1½ teaspoons dried thyme)

FOR ASSEMBLY

1 recipe Basic Pastry and Biscuit Dough (page 186)
5 ounces sharp Cheddar cheese, grated
Egg wash (1 egg beaten with 1 tablespoon milk)

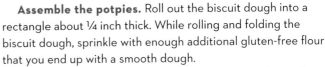

MAKE-AHEAD OPTION: The pasties can be shaped and filled, raw, then placed in a single layer on a baking sheet and frozen. Pile them into a freezer-safe bag and return them to the freezer. Bake them from frozen after brushing with the egg wash, and simply add a couple of minutes to the baking time as necessary. Once fully prepared, they are best eaten right away.

BIGGER BITE OPTION: Shape the rounds of dough to 5½ inches in diameter, then roll out to 6 inches. Double the filling and other ingredients in each, and proceed with the recipe as written. Increase the baking time to about 20 minutes.

Assemble the potpies. Roll out the biscuit dough into a rectangle about ¼ inch thick. While rolling and folding the biscuit dough, sprinkle with enough additional gluten-free flour that you end up with a smooth dough.

Place a small fingerbowl of lukewarm water beside you for moistening the edges of the dough. With a 3-inch round biscuit or cookie cutter, cut out rounds of dough. Sprinkle them lightly with more flour and roll into 3½-inch rounds. Gather and reroll scraps. Separate the rounds from one another and place about 1 teaspoon of the filling on the bottom half of each round, leaving about ½ inch clean at the edge. Top with about 1 table-spoon of chopped chicken, then with another small dollop of filling and about 2 teaspoons grated cheese. Moisten the edges of each round with a wet finger, and fold the dough in half to enclose the filling, gently pressing out the air as you fold. Press the edges to seal and, using a sharp knife or pastry cutter, slice three vents on top of each pasty. Place the pasties 1 inch apart from one another on the prepared baking sheets, and place in the freezer until firm, about 5 minutes.

Remove the chilled pasties from the freezer and brush each generously with the egg wash. Place in the center of the preheated oven, and bake until they're puffed and pale golden all over and more brown around the edges, about 10 minutes. Remove from the oven and allow to cool slightly before serving warm.

miniature shepherd's pies

IF YOU EVER FIND YOURSELF WITH LEFTOVER MASHED potatoes, say from Potato Skins (page 68), and don't feel much like making croquettes (page 41), these miniature shepherd's pies are the way to go. The recipe provides instructions for making mashed potatoes from scratch, but if you are using leftovers, you'll need about 1¼ cups mashed. Our favorite pastry and biscuit dough makes a perfect light and flaky crust, the beef and vegetable filling is warm and comforting, and the Cheddar mashed potatoes are everything you could hope for. The ultimate comfort food—in handheld form.

Preheat your oven to 375°F. Grease the wells of a standard 12-cup muffin tin and set it aside.

If you're using leftover mashed potatoes, skip to the next step. Make the mashed potatoes. Place the potatoes, with the skins still on, in a large pot and cover with cold, salted water by about 2 inches. Cover the pot, bring to a boil over medium heat, and allow to cook for about 30 minutes, or until the potatoes are just fork-tender. Remove from the heat and drain the water. While the potatoes are still warm, remove the skins and pass the potatoes through a ricer or food mill or mash completely with a fork. Add the butter and milk, and mix until well combined and smooth.

To the mashed potatoes (either just made or leftover), add the salt and 2 ounces of the shredded Cheddar cheese, and mix until smooth.

Place the biscuit dough on a lightly floured surface and sprinkle lightly with more flour. Roll out into a rectangle about ¼ inch thick, and cut out 5-inch rounds from the dough. To the extent it is reasonable to do so without working the dough too much and melting the butter, gather and reroll the scraps of biscuit dough. Press each of the rounds of dough into the bottom and up the sides of the greased muffin tin. Using the tines of a fork, pierce two sets of holes in the bottom of the biscuit dough in each well. Place in the center of the preheated oven and bake for 7 to 10 minutes, or until the pastry dough is just beginning to brown. Remove from the oven and set the pastry shells aside to cool.

FOR THE MASHED POTATOES

1 pound Yukon Gold potatoes
2 tablespoons (28 g) unsalted butter, at room temperature
¼ cup (2 fluid ounces) milk, at room temperature
¼ teaspoon kosher salt
3 ounces sharp yellow Cheddar, shredded, divided
1 recipe Basic Pastry and Biscuit Dough (page 186), chilled

FOR THE FILLING

2 tablespoons (28 g) extra-virgin olive oil
1 small yellow onion, peeled and diced
¾ pound 90% lean ground beef
½ cup (4 fluid ounces) beef stock
2 tablespoons (18 g) Basic Gum-Free Gluten-Free Flour (page 4)
1 teaspoon dried oregano
¼ teaspoon kosher salt
⅛ teaspoon freshly ground black pepper
1½ cups frozen mixed vegetables, defrosted and drained of any liquid
1 tablespoon unsalted butter, melted

—⚓︎—

MAKE-AHEAD OPTION: The mashed potatoes in the first step can be made up to 3 days ahead of time and stored in the refrigerator. The pastry shells can be shaped and frozen in a stack, then wrapped tightly and stored in the freezer for up to 2 months. Allow to defrost slightly in the refrigerator before pressing into the wells of a muffin tin, or the dough will crack. Once fully prepared, these are best eaten right away.

BIGGER BITE OPTION: Rather than making individual miniature pies, this can be made as one traditional large shepherd's pie. Grease a standard 9-inch pie plate, and prepare the pastry crust so that it forms about a 10-inch round. Lay the piecrust on top of the prepared pie plate, and press it gently into the bottom and up the sides. Trim any irregular overhung edges of the pastry, and fold the crust under so that it's flush with the edge of the pie plate. Crimp the edge to seal. Cover the piecrust with a piece of unbleached parchment paper, and place pie weights or dried beans in the center. Parbake the crust at 375°F for about 12 minutes, or until just beginning to brown. Remove from the oven, remove the paper and the pie weights, and set the crust aside to cool. Make the filling and the Cheddar mashed potatoes as instructed, and assemble them into one pie in the parbaked crust. Place in the center of the preheated oven, and bake until the mashed potatoes are lightly golden brown on top, about 25 minutes. Allow to set at room temperature before slicing and serving.

—⚓︎—

In a large, heavy-bottomed skillet, heat the olive oil over medium heat. Add the onion and sauté, stirring frequently, until the onion is translucent, about 6 minutes. Add the ground beef and break it up with a spatula or fork. Cook, stirring occasionally, until no pink remains. In a small bowl, place the stock and add the flour, oregano, salt, and pepper, whisk until the flour dissolves into the stock, and pour the mixture into the skillet with the onions and ground beef. Cook, stirring frequently, until the liquid is absorbed.

Fill the baked pastry shells each with about ¼ cup of the beef mixture, then top with 1 tablespoon of the mixed vegetables and about ¼ cup of the mashed potatoes, and smooth with a wet spatula. Brush the tops of the mashed potatoes with the melted butter, sprinkling with the remaining 1 ounce of shredded Cheddar cheese, and place in the center of the preheated oven. Bake for 15 minutes or until the mashed potatoes are lightly golden brown on top. Remove from the oven and allow to cool for 10 minutes before running a butter knife along the edge of each muffin well to loosen the pies. Remove the pies and serve immediately.

chapter 7: sweet endings

sugar cookie cups

MAKE A BATCH OF SUGAR COOKIES FOR FRIENDS AND family, and they'll no doubt enjoy them (especially because you have the best recipe). But make a batch of these sweet, chewy little sugar cookie cups and fill them simply with berries and cream, or maybe with some chocolate ganache (see recipe below), topped with a spoonful of whipped cream, and now you're a conquering hero.

Preheat your oven to 350°F. Grease well a standard 12-cup muffin tin and set it aside.

In a large bowl, place the flour, baking powder, salt, confectioners' sugar, and granulated sugar, and whisk to combine well. Create a well in the center of the dry ingredients and add the butter, shortening, egg, and vanilla, mixing well to combine after each addition. The dough should come together and will be soft. Roll the dough into balls about 1¼ inches in diameter, and press into disks about ¼ inch thick. Place one disk into each of the prepared wells of the muffin tin, and press the bottom of a juice glass right into the center of the dough, forcing the dough evenly up the sides of each well. Remove the glass. If any of the cookie has reached above the lip of each well, press it down to avoid it burning in the oven. Using a toothpick, poke three evenly spaced holes in the bottom of the dough in each well.

Place in the center of the preheated oven and bake for 12 minutes, or until the edges are very lightly golden brown and the center of each cup springs back when pressed gently. Remove from the oven and allow to cool for 5 minutes, before carefully transferring the cups to a wire rack to cool completely. Repeat with the remaining few pieces of cookie dough. Serve filled with cream and berries or chocolate ganache (see sidebar for instructions).

MAKES 12 CUPS

1¾ cups (245 g) all-purpose gluten-free flour (page 2)
½ teaspoon baking powder
½ teaspoon kosher salt
½ cup (58 g) confectioners' sugar
½ cup (100 g) granulated sugar
5 tablespoons (70 g) unsalted butter, at room temperature
5 tablespoons (60 g) vegetable shortening, melted and cooled
1 egg (50 g, weighed out of shell), at room temperature, beaten
2 teaspoons pure vanilla extract

FOR SERVING

Whipped cream and berries
Ganache

MAKE-AHEAD OPTION: The shells can easily be made ahead of time, but they must stored in a hard-sided, sealed container in well-defined layers, rather than wrapped in plastic wrap or piled into a zip-top bag, or they'll crack. They will keep in a sealed container at room temperature for about 5 days, or wrapped tightly and frozen for longer storage, then defrosted at room temperature.

CHOCOLATE GANACHE OPTION: To make a simple chocolate ganache, heat ¾ cup (6 fluid ounces) heavy whipping cream in a small, heavy-bottomed saucepan until it just begins to simmer. Place 8 ounces of chopped chocolate in a medium-size bowl, and pour the hot cream over the chocolate. Allow the cream to sit on the chocolate for about a minute, until the chocolate begins to melt, and mix until the chocolate is melted and the mixture is smooth and glossy. Pour into the cooled sugar cookie cups and allow to set at room temperature.

peanut butter cookie chips

MAKES ABOUT 100 COOKIE
CHIPS

1¼ cups (320 g) smooth no-stir peanut
  butter

5 tablespoons (70 g) unsalted butter,
  chopped

1⅓ cups (187 g) all-purpose gluten-free
  flour (page 2), plus more for sprinkling

2½ tablespoons (23 g) cornstarch

1 teaspoon baking soda

¼ teaspoon kosher salt

1 cup (200 g) granulated sugar

2 egg whites (50 g), at room temperature

1 teaspoon pure vanilla extract

2 tablespoons (1 fluid ounce) milk, at room
  temperature

———————— ⚜ ————————

MAKE-AHEAD OPTION: They're cookies!
Of course you can make them ahead. To
maintain crispness, store them in a sealed
glass (not plastic!) container at room temperature. They can be frozen for longer
storage, but if you pack these super crispy
cookie chips too tightly, or they move
around too much when they're stored, they
will break.

BIGGER BITE OPTION: Make cookies that
are double the size by cutting out shapes
with a larger cookie cutter. Baking time
will need to be increased by about 2 to 4
minutes, depending upon size.

———————— ⚜ ————————

CRISPY, CRUNCHY PEANUT BUTTER COOKIE CHIPS
*are not only perfect for popping one after another in your mouth,
but they make an amazing base for a peanut butter crumb piecrust (like a graham cracker crust, but peanut butter instead!).
Or try crumbling some of them over a scoop of vanilla ice cream.
You will need a smooth, no-stir peanut butter variety for this
recipe. No-stir peanut butter is just the commercial kind that's
processed enough so that the oil doesn't separate in the jar, so
you don't have to stir it upon opening. The true "natural" peanut
butters won't work here.*

Preheat your oven to 350°F. Line rimmed baking sheets with
unbleached parchment paper and set aside.

In a medium-size, heat-safe bowl, place the peanut butter
and butter, and melt in the microwave in 30-second bursts, stirring in between, until melted and smooth. Alternatively, melt the
peanut butter and butter in a small, heavy-bottomed saucepan
over low heat until melted and smooth. Set the peanut butter
mixture aside to cool briefly. In a large bowl, place the flour,
cornstarch, baking soda, salt, and granulated sugar, and whisk to
combine well. Create a well in the center of the dry ingredients,
and add the peanut butter mixture, then the egg whites, vanilla,
and milk, mixing to combine after each addition. The cookie
dough will be thick but soft.

Place the cookie dough on a large sheet of unbleached
parchment paper sprinkled lightly with flour. Sprinkle the top
lightly with more flour, and roll out the cookie dough as close to
⅛ inch thick as possible. Using a round 1½-inch cookie cutter,
cut out shapes as close as possible to one another. Peel away
the excess cookie dough around the shapes, and then peel the
parchment paper away from the cookies to transfer them to
the baking sheet, placed 1 inch apart from one another, without
stretching out the shapes. Place the baking sheets, one at a
time, in the center of the preheated oven and bake until lightly
golden brown all over and just firm to the touch, about 10
minutes. Remove from the oven and cool for about 5 minutes on
the baking sheet.

Peanut Butter Cookie Chips (page 152), Chocolate Chip Cookie Chips (page 155), and Snickerdoodle Cookie Chips (page 154)

snickerdoodle cookie chips

MAKES ABOUT 40 COOKIE CHIPS

1 cup plus 2 tablespoons (158 g) all-
    purpose gluten-free flour (page 2)

2 tablespoons (18 g) cornstarch

1 teaspoon baking soda

1 teaspoon cream of tartar

¼ teaspoon kosher salt

1½ teaspoons ground cinnamon

⅞ cup (175 g) sugar

8 tablespoons (112 g) unsalted butter,
    melted and cooled

1 egg white (25 g), at room temperature

1 tablespoon (21 g) unsulfured molasses

2 teaspoons pure vanilla extract

1½ tablespoons ground cinnamon

3 tablespoons (36 g) sugar

MAKE-AHEAD OPTION: They're cookies! Of course you can make them ahead. To maintain crispness, store them in a sealed glass (not plastic!) container at room temperature. They can be frozen for longer storage, but if you pack these super crispy cookie chips too tightly, or they move around too much when they're stored, they'll break.

BIGGER BITE OPTION: Make cookies that are double the size by increasing each portion to 1½-inch balls of dough (about 1 tablespoon each). Use the same method for making the dough superthin on the baking sheet, and be sure to keep the cookies 2 inches apart from one another. Baking time will need to be increased by about 2 to 4 minutes, depending on size.

THESE PARTICULAR COOKIE CHIPS ARE JUST AS addictive as all the others (see pages 152, 155), and surprisingly satisfying to a snickerdoodle lover. Typically, these cinnamon-sugar cookies, made with cream of tartar for the perfect tang, are gorgeously chewy. But these are impossibly thin cookie chips, so in spite of the cream of tartar, they snap and crumble a bit when you bite into them, like chips. Trying is believing.

Preheat your oven to 350°F. Line rimmed baking sheets with unbleached parchment paper and set aside.

In a large bowl, place the flour, cornstarch, baking soda, cream of tartar, salt, ground cinnamon, and sugar, and whisk to combine well. Create a well in the center of the dry ingredients, and add the butter, egg white, molasses, and vanilla, mixing to combine after each addition. The cookie dough will be thick but soft.

Pull off pieces of cookie dough and roll into balls about ¾ inch in diameter. Combine the cinnamon and sugar for the topping in a small bowl, and place each ball of cookie dough in the cinnamon-sugar. Flatten into the cinnamon-sugar until the ball is a disk about 1½ inches in diameter, coating the disk well with cinnamon-sugar on both sides. Place the disks 1½ inches apart from one another on the prepared baking sheets. Place in the center of the preheated oven and bake for 6 to 8 minutes, or until the cookies are lightly golden brown all over. Remove from the oven and allow to cool on the baking sheet for 5 minutes before transferring to a wire rack to cool completely. The cookies will crisp as they cool.

chocolate chip cookie chips

YOU KNOW HOW YOU REALLY CAN'T EAT JUST ONE potato chip, which is, of course, their greatest blessing and greatest curse? So it goes with cookie chips. They're just so crispy and popable! My favorite of the three varieties in this book (see pages 152 and 154) is undoubtedly the chocolate chippers. They're just so classic, with the light molasses taste, the perfect crispness and, of course, the miniature chocolate chips. It's like a whole cookie that tastes entirely like the crispy edges of a "regular" chocolate chip cookie. If you're a soft chocolate chip sort of person, no worries (page 156).

Preheat your oven to 350°F. Line rimmed baking sheets with unbleached parchment paper and set aside.

In a large bowl, place the flour, cornstarch, baking soda, salt, and granulated sugar, and whisk to combine well. Create a well in the center of the dry ingredients, and add the butter, egg white, molasses, and vanilla, mixing to combine after each addition. The cookie dough will be thick but soft. Add the miniature chocolate chips tossed with cornstarch, and mix until the chips are evenly distributed throughout the dough.

Roll the cookie dough into balls about ¾ inch in diameter (about 1½ teaspoons of dough each), and place 2 inches apart from one another on the prepared baking sheets. Pat each ball of cookie dough into a very flat disk on the baking sheet, until each is no thicker than the miniature chocolate chips in the dough (about ⅛ inch thick). Place the baking sheets, one at a time, in the center of the preheated oven, and bake until golden brown all over and just firm to the touch, about 9 minutes. Remove from the oven and cool for about 5 minutes on the baking sheet.

MAKES ABOUT 40 COOKIE CHIPS

1 cup plus 2 tablespoons (158 g) all-purpose gluten-free flour (page 2)

2 tablespoons (18 g) cornstarch

½ teaspoon baking soda

¼ teaspoon kosher salt

⅞ cup (175 g) granulated sugar

8 tablespoons (112 g) unsalted butter, melted and cooled

1 egg white (25 g), at room temperature

½ tablespoon (10 g) unsulfured molasses

2 teaspoons pure vanilla extract

3 ounces miniature semisweet chocolate chips, tossed with 1 teaspoon cornstarch

———————— ⚜ ————————

MAKE-AHEAD OPTION: They're cookies! Of course you can make them ahead. To maintain crispness, store them in a sealed glass (not plastic!) container at room temperature. They can be frozen for longer storage, but if you pack these super crispy cookie chips too tightly, or they can move around too much when they're stored, they will break.

BIGGER BITE OPTION: Make cookies that are double the size by increasing each portion to 1½-inch balls of dough (about 1 tablespoon each). Use the same method for making the dough superthin on the baking sheet, and be sure to keep the cookies 2 inches apart from one another. Baking time will need to be increased by about 2 to 4 minutes, depending on size.

———————— ⚘ ————————

soft chocolate chip cookie bites

2 cups (280 g) all-purpose gluten-free flour (page 2)

¼ cup plus 1 tablespoon (45 g) cornstarch

½ teaspoon kosher salt

1 teaspoon baking soda

6 ounces miniature semisweet chocolate chips

¾ cup (150 g) granulated sugar

6 tablespoons (82 g) packed light-brown sugar

10 tablespoons (140 g) unsalted butter, at room temperature

2 eggs (100 g, weighed out of shell), at room temperature, beaten

1 tablespoon pure vanilla extract

MAKE-AHEAD OPTION: Make them almost as far ahead as you like, but just wrap them well, sealing out all air to prevent freezer burn, and freeze. Defrost at room temperature.

BIGGER BITE OPTION: Go on and double the size if you like! Otherwise, follow the directions as written but add about 4 minutes to the baking time, depending upon size.

AS PROMISED, MINIATURE SOFT CHOCOLATE CHIP cookies. Because I've never met a person who didn't enjoy a nice chocolate chipper, but there is most definitely room for disagreement on the topic of perfect texture. These are the thicker, soft-baked chocolate chip cookies that always manage to taste like they just came out of the oven, made mini.

Preheat your oven to 325°F. Line rimmed baking sheets with unbleached parchment paper, and set them aside.

In a large bowl, place the flour, cornstarch, salt, and baking soda, and whisk to combine well. Place the chocolate chips in a separate small bowl, add about 1 teaspoonful of the dry ingredients, and toss to coat. Set the chips aside. To the bowl of dry ingredients, add the granulated sugar and the light-brown sugar, and whisk to combine well, working out any lumps in the brown sugar. Create a well in the center of the dry ingredients, and add the butter, eggs, and vanilla, mixing to combine well after each addition. The dough will be thick and soft. Add the chips tossed with the teaspoonful of dry ingredients, and mix until evenly distributed throughout the dough.

Drop the dough by the teaspoonful on the prepared baking sheets, about 2 inches apart from one another. Roll each piece of dough tightly into a ball and replace on the baking sheets. Place the baking sheets in the refrigerator or freezer to chill until firm (about 1 hour in the refrigerator, or 10 minutes in the freezer).

Once the dough has chilled, place in the center of the preheated oven and bake for 8 minutes, or just until the balls of dough have melted and spread and the cookies are set in the center. They will be very lightly brown around the edges, and some may even be slightly wet toward the center. Remove from the oven and allow to cool for at least 10 minutes on the baking sheet before transferring to a wire rack to cool completely.

chocolate chip cookie dough truffles

I'M NOT EXACTLY SURE WHEN THE WHOLE EDIBLE cookie dough phenomenon started, but I am proud to say that I have been able to appreciate it without ever going overboard. These cookie dough truffles are our ticket to guilt-free cookie dough eating, and although they're heaven when coated with chocolate, they're also delicious frozen nude and then mixed into some vanilla ice cream before it's frozen. Ben & Jerry, here we come!

Make the cookie dough. Line a small rimmed baking sheet with waxed paper, and set it aside. In a large bowl, place the flour, xanthan gum, salt, and granulated sugar, and whisk to combine well. Add the brown sugar, and whisk again, working out any lumps. Create a well in the center of the dry ingredients, and add the butter, vanilla, and 1 tablespoon of milk, mixing to combine after each addition. Knead the dough together with your hands, adding more milk by the ¼ teaspoonful as necessary for the dough to hold together without crumbling. Add the miniature chocolate chips and mix until evenly distributed throughout the dough.

Divide the cookie dough into about 18 pieces, each about 1½ teaspoons. Roll each tightly into a ball and place on the prepared baking sheet in a single layer. Place in the freezer until firm (about 10 minutes) before coating in chocolate.

Prepare the glaze and dip the truffles. In a medium-size, microwave-safe bowl, place the chocolate and coconut oil and microwave in 30-second increments at 70% power, stirring in between. Alternatively, place the chocolate in a small, heat-safe bowl over a double boiler and stir gently until melted. Add the vanilla, and mix to incorporate. Allow the chocolate to sit at room temperature until it begins to thicken a bit. Remove the truffles from the freezer and immerse them, one at a time, in the glaze. Press down on the truffle with the tines of a fork, then flip it gently in the chocolate. Pull it out of the chocolate by slipping the fork under it and bobbing the truffle on the surface of the chocolate a few times before pulling it along the edge of the bowl and carefully placing it back on the prepared baking sheet. Allow the chocolate glaze to set at room temperature.

MAKES 18 TRUFFLES

FOR THE COOKIE DOUGH

½ cup plus 1 tablespoon (79 g) Basic Gum-Free Gluten-Free Flour (page 4)
⅛ teaspoon xanthan gum
⅛ teaspoon kosher salt
3 tablespoons (36 g) granulated sugar
3 tablespoons (40 g) packed light-brown sugar
2 tablespoons (28 g) unsalted butter, at room temperature
1 teaspoon pure vanilla extract
1 to 2 tablespoons milk, at room temperature
1½ ounces miniature semisweet chocolate chips

FOR THE CHOCOLATE GLAZE

8 ounces dark chocolate, chopped
2 tablespoons (28 g) virgin coconut oil
½ teaspoon pure vanilla extract

MAKE-AHEAD OPTION: These truffles can certainly be made ahead of time. Make and shape the cookie dough, then freeze it in a single layer on a rimmed baking sheet before piling into a freezer-safe zip-topped bag and return to the freezer. Coat with chocolate according to the recipe instructions without defrosting. Once coated in chocolate, the truffles can also be kept on hand, although the chocolate may bloom over time, affecting the appearance but not the taste.

BIGGER BITE OPTION: These truffles can be made any size you like!

Chocolate Chip Cookie Dough Truffles (page 157) and Chocolate Cookie Dough Truffles (page 159)

chocolate cookie dough truffles

THESE RICH, CHOCOLATE TRUFFLES ARE SO EASY—NO baking required. Replace the vanilla extract with mint or orange extract, and completely change the flavor profile. Just be sure to work with wet dough during shaping, and allow the shaped truffles to dry before coating them in chocolate. If you use natural unsweetened cocoa powder, add ⅛ teaspoon baking soda to the dry ingredients.

In a medium-size, microwave-safe bowl, place the butter and chocolate and melt in the microwave in 30-second increments at 70% power, stirring in between. Alternatively, place the chocolate and butter in a small, heat-safe bowl over a double boiler and stir gently until melted. Stir in the vanilla, and set the bowl aside. In a large bowl, place the flour, cocoa powder, salt, and sugar, and whisk to combine well. Create a well in the center of the dry ingredients, add the melted chocolate mixture, and mix to combine. Knead the dough together, adding water by the ¼ teaspoonful as necessary to bring the dough together, and make sure that it is pliable and not stiff.

Line a large baking sheet with parchment paper and set it aside. Using a small ice-cream scoop (a #70 scoop is perfect, equal to 1 tablespoon) or two spoons, scoop out mounds of the cookie dough and place about 1 inch apart from one another. Roll each mound of dough tightly into a round between your palms and replace on the baking sheet. Allow to sit at room temperature until the truffles are firm, about 1 hour. This will make it much easier to dip them in the chocolate glaze.

In a medium-size, microwave-safe bowl, place the chocolate and coconut oil and microwave in 30-second increments at 70% power, stirring in between. Alternatively, place the chocolate and coconut oil in a small, heat-safe bowl over a double boiler and stir gently until melted. Add the vanilla, and mix. Allow the chocolate to sit at room temperature until it begins to thicken a bit. Immerse the truffles, one at a time, in the glaze. Press down on the truffle with the tines of a fork, then flip it gently in the chocolate. Pull it out of the chocolate by slipping the fork under it and bobbing the truffle on the surface of the chocolate a few times before pulling it along the edge of the bowl. Allow to set at room temperature.

FOR THE COOKIE DOUGH

5 tablespoons (70 g) unsalted butter, chopped

4 ounces semisweet chocolate, chopped

½ teaspoon pure vanilla extract

¾ cup (105 g) all-purpose gluten-free flour (page 2)

½ cup (40 g) unsweetened cocoa powder

½ teaspoon kosher salt

½ cup (100 g) granulated sugar

Warm water by the ¼ teaspoonful, as necessary

FOR THE CHOCOLATE GLAZE

8 ounces dark chocolate, chopped

2 tablespoons (28 g) virgin coconut oil

½ teaspoon pure vanilla extract

MAKE-AHEAD OPTION: These truffles can certainly be made ahead of time. Make and shape the cookie dough, then freeze it in a single layer on a rimmed baking sheet before piling into a freezer-safe zip-topped bag and return to the freezer. Coat with chocolate according to the recipe instructions without defrosting. Once coated in chocolate, the truffles can also be kept on hand, although the chocolate may bloom over time, affecting the appearance but not the taste.

BIGGER BITE OPTION: These truffles can be made any size you like!

sopapillas

AS MANY TIMES AS I'VE MADE THESE LITTLE SWEET dough gems, I'm surprised and delighted every time they "pop" in the frying oil. My favorite way to enjoy them is to bite off an end, then drizzle extra honey right into the pocket moments before that satisfying first crunch. Sadly, there isn't a no-fry option for these. Baking will not cause them to pop.

In a large bowl, place the flour, Expandex, salt, baking powder, and sugar, and whisk to combine well. Create a well in the center of the dry ingredients, add the melted shortening or oil, milk, and water, and mix to combine until the dough comes together. Squeeze the dough together into a ball. It should hold together well and not be so stiff that it is hard to knead. If it is hard to knead, add more water by the teaspoonful, kneading it in after each addition, until the dough is pliable but still holds together very well. Transfer the dough to a large piece of plastic wrap, and wrap tightly. Allow to rest at room temperature for 15 minutes.

Unwrap the dough, divide it into 7 equal portions, and form each into a ball. On a large, flat surface, roll each dough ball with a rolling pin into a round about 6 inches in diameter and ¼ inch thick. Cut off the rough edges with a 6-inch cake cutter; the lid of a pot in the proper size should work, too. It is important to roll the dough out very evenly, and for each round to have very clean, well-defined edges. This helps the sopapillas to puff up during frying. Using a pizza or pastry wheel, or a very sharp knife, slice each round carefully into 4 quarters.

Place paper towels on a plate, and set it aside. Place 2 inches of oil in a heavy-bottomed saucepan or deep fryer, and bring the oil to 375°F. Place the quarters of dough in the hot oil, taking care not to crowd them. Within the first few seconds, the dough rounds should float to the top and expand as they fill with air. As soon as they "pop," turn them over using tongs or chopsticks, and fry until lightly golden brown on both sides (30 to 45 seconds per side). Remove the dough from the oil, and place on the paper-towel-lined plate to drain. Bring the oil back to temperature between batches. Serve warm, with a drizzle of honey.

MAKES ABOUT 28 SOPAPILLAS

1 ¾ cups (245 g) all-purpose gluten-free flour (page 2)

¼ cup (36 g) Expandex modified tapioca starch (page 3)

1 teaspoon kosher salt

2 teaspoons baking powder

2 teaspoons (8 g) sugar

2 tablespoons (28 g) vegetable shortening, melted, or neutral oil (like canola or vegetable oil)

¼ cup (2 fluid ounces) milk, at room temperature

½ cup (4 fluid ounces) lukewarm water, plus more by the teaspoonful, as necessary

Neutral oil, for frying

Honey, for serving

MAKE-AHEAD OPTION: The raw dough for these can be made into rounds and frozen in a stack, uncut and wrapped tightly, for up to 2 months. Defrost briefly at room temperature and blot dry before continuing with the rest of the recipe instructions. Once fried, these are best eaten right away.

easy palmiers

MAKES 24 PALMIERS

1 recipe Basic Pastry and Biscuit Dough
  (page 186), chilled
1 cup (200 g) granulated sugar
¼ teaspoon kosher salt
1 egg white (25 g)

PALMIERS (IF YOU'RE FANCY) OR ELEPHANT EARS (IF you're feeling state fair-ish) are typically made using puff pastry dough and not biscuit dough, but these are "easy" palmiers, and if you make the dough and then the cookies as directed, I challenge you to detect a difference. The main difference between traditional puff pastry and our Basic Pastry and Biscuit Dough (page 186) is that puff pastry begins with a large butter packet, rather than chunks of cold butter, that is painstakingly laminated into pastry dough, multiplying the layers of pastry visible upon baking. If you count the layers, we might be missing a few, but you won't mind when you're enjoying a delightfully sweet, extra-flaky cookie with your afternoon tea, you fancy thing you.

Prepare the biscuit dough according to the recipe instructions.

Mix the sugar and salt in a separate, medium-size bowl, until well combined. Sprinkle ⅓ cup (67 g) of the sugar and salt mixture on a large, flat surface, such as a large pastry board, cutting board, or smooth countertop, and spread into an even, rectangular layer (about 16 inches by 14 inches in area). Place the chilled biscuit dough on top of the sugar mixture, sprinkle lightly with flour, and roll into a rectangle that is about 16 inches by 14 inches, and a bit more than ⅛ inch thick. Trim any irregular edges of the rectangle with a pastry cutter, pizza wheel, or very sharp knife. Brush the entire top of the pastry rectangle with the egg white in a thin, even layer. Sprinkle another ⅓ cup (67 g) of the sugar mixture on top of the pastry dough rectangle, spread into an even layer, and press down gently to help the sugar adhere to the dough. Gently fold each 16-inch side of the pastry rectangle one-quarter of the way toward the center. Fold the same sides again, another quarter of the way toward the center so that they meet in the middle. Finally, fold both edges of the now 8-inch rectangle along the center seam over one another, creating a 14 x 4-inch rectangle with 6 distinct layers of dough. Place the entire rectangle on the prepared baking sheet, and then in the freezer for 10 minutes or until firm.

Once the dough is firm, remove from the freezer and transfer the dough to a cutting board. Using a very sharp knife, slice the dough by cross-section into 24 equal pieces, each about ½ inch wide. Dip both sides of each piece in the remaining

⅓ cup (67 g) of sugar mixture, and then place on the prepared baking sheets, about 2 inches apart from one another. Press the flat bottom of a glass firmly and evenly onto the top of each of the cookies on the baking sheet to compress the layers by about one-quarter. Place in the freezer for about 5 minutes, or until once again firm.

One at a time, place the baking sheets in the preheated oven for 9 minutes, or until the cookies are lightly golden brown on the underside. Working quickly, remove the baking sheet from the oven, and carefully flip each cookie over. Return to the oven and bake for another 3 to 4 minutes, or until lightly golden brown on the second side. Remove from the oven and allow to cool on the baking sheet for 5 minutes before transferring to a wire rack to cool completely.

glazed donut holes

THESE TENDER, LIGHT-AS-AIR DONUT HOLES, WITH the perfect sugar glaze that crackles when you bite into it, are the perfect way to finish any get-together. In fact, I think they're the ideal sweet ending to a delightful Sunday brunch with friends and family. After all, it's not a "whole donut." It's just the hole. This traditional yeasted donut recipe calls for two rises, but most of the time is inactive time—and these tender bites are worth the extra step! Once fully prepared, these are best eaten right away.

First, make the donut dough. In the bowl of your stand mixer, place the flour, cream of tartar, yeast, and sugar, and use a handheld whisk to combine well. Add the salt and nutmeg, and whisk to combine well. Add the milk, egg, and butter, and mix on low speed with the dough hook until combined. Raise the mixer speed to medium, and knead for about 5 minutes. This is a lovely, smooth, and supple enriched dough. It climbs up the dough hook during kneading but remains intact and smooth. Spray a silicone spatula lightly with cooking oil spray, and use it to scrape down the sides of the bowl. Transfer the dough to a lightly oiled bowl or proofing bucket large enough for it to rise to double its size, spray the top of the dough with cooking oil spray, and cover with a piece of oiled plastic wrap or the oiled top of your proofing bucket. Place the dough in a warm, draft-free location to rise to about double its size, about 1½ hours. Place the risen dough in the refrigerator to chill for about 30 minutes. This will make handling the dough much easier.

Once the dough has undergone its first rise, remove it from the refrigerator, uncover it, and turn out the chilled dough onto a lightly floured surface. Sprinkle the dough lightly with more flour and knead it lightly by scraping the dough off the floured surface with a floured bench scraper or bowl scraper, then folding it over on itself. Repeat scraping and folding until the dough has become smoother. Do not overwork the dough or you will incorporate too much flour into it and it will not rise properly. Sprinkle the dough once more lightly with flour, then roll it out into a rectangle about 1 inch thick. With a floured round cookie cutter about 1 inch in diameter, cut out rounds of dough, and place each piece on a greased, parchment-lined baking sheet. Cover with lightly oiled plastic wrap, and set in a

MAKES ABOUT 36 DONUT HOLES

FOR THE DONUT DOUGH

3 cups (420 g) Gluten-Free Bread Flour (page 4), plus more for sprinkling

¼ teaspoon cream of tartar

2 teaspoons (6 g) instant yeast

½ cup (100 g) granulated sugar

½ teaspoon (3 g) kosher salt

½ teaspoon fresh finely grated nutmeg

¾ cup plus 2 tablespoons (7 fluid ounces) warm milk (about 95°F) (not nonfat)

1 egg (50 g, weighed out of shell), at room temperature, beaten

4 tablespoons (56 g) unsalted butter, melted and cooled

Neutral oil, for frying

FOR THE GLAZE

1 cup (115 g) confectioners' sugar

1 tablespoon milk (any kind), plus more by the ¼ teaspoonful, as necessary

warm, draft-free location to rise for 30 minutes, or until puffed but not doubled.

As the dough is nearing the end of its rise, place about 3 inches of frying oil in a medium-size, heavy-bottomed pot or fryer, and bring the oil temperature to 350°F over medium-high heat. Place the raised donut holes a few at a time in the hot oil, taking care not to crowd the oil. Fry until very lightly golden brown all over (2 to 3 minutes per side). As soon as each batch is removed from the fryer, place on a wire rack placed over paper towels to drain and cool completely. Bring the oil back to temperature between batches.

While the donut holes are cooling, make the glaze. In a small bowl, place the confectioners' sugar and 1 tablespoon of milk. Mix well, until a thick paste forms. Add more milk by the ¼ teaspoon, mixing to combine well, until the glaze falls off the spoon slowly, in a thick but pourable glaze. Add milk very slowly, as it is much easier to thin, than to thicken, the glaze. If you do thin the glaze too much, add more confectioners' sugar a teaspoon at a time to thicken it. Immerse each cooled donut hole in the glaze, and lift out with the tines of a fork or chocolate dipping tool, and return to the wire rack for any excess glaze to drip off. Allow the glaze to set at room temperature and serve immediately.

NO-FRY OPTION: These are not the ideal donuts to bake, instead of fry, as they are yeasted donuts. However, they *can* be baked. They will just taste more like sweet rolls than they do donuts. Simply proof the donuts as described in the recipe instructions, then brush with an egg wash (1 egg beaten with 1 tablespoon milk), and bake at 350°F until puffed and lightly golden brown all over, about 20 minutes. Remove from the oven and cool for about 5 minutes on the baking sheet before transferring to a wire rack to cool. Glaze as directed.

BIGGER BITE OPTION: This very same recipe can be used to make full-size, traditional donuts. Rather than cutting out 1-inch rounds of dough with a wee little cookie cutter, either use a full-size donut cutter, or cut out larger rounds using a 3-inch round cookie cutter, and use the 1-inch cookie cutter to cut out a donut hole. Fry as directed, but increase the frying time by about 3 minutes per batch.

bear claws

BEAR CLAWS, SO NAMED BECAUSE WE GIVE THEM
"toes" that resemble, well, bear claws, are sweet, delicate pastries
traditionally made with Danish pastry dough, which is a yeasted
puff pastry. Similar to how we simplified palmiers (page 162), here
we make bear claws with the same tried-and-true biscuit and
pastry dough that's served us so well time and again. But it's
the tender, flaky pastry outside and the sweet and spicy cinna-
mon-almond filling that are really what make bear claws special.

MAKES 12 BEAR CLAWS

1 recipe Basic Pastry and Biscuit Dough
 (page 186), chilled
½ cup (130 g) gluten-free almond paste,
 broken up into small pieces
1 egg white (25 g), at room temperature
¼ cup (29 g) confectioners' sugar
1 teaspoon ground cinnamon
Egg wash (1 egg beaten with 1 tablespoon
 milk)
Slivered almonds, for decorating

MAKE-AHEAD OPTION: This dough can
be shaped, filled, and divided into 12 raw
pastries ahead of time, then frozen on
a baking sheet before being wrapped
tightly and returned to the freezer. I don't
recommend slicing the "toes" into each
raw pastry for this make-ahead option.
Allow to defrost in the refrigerator before
shaping the toes and fanning the pastries
out, or the pastry will crack. Bake chilled.
Once fully prepared, these are best eaten
right away.

Preheat your oven to 375°F. Prepare the biscuit dough according to the recipe instructions. Line a large rimmed baking sheet
with unbleached parchment paper and set it aside.

Place the pastry dough on a lightly floured surface, sprinkle
lightly with flour, and roll into a rectangle that is about 12 inches
by 8 inches and a bit less than ¼ inch thick. Trim any irregular
edges of the rectangle with a pastry cutter, pizza wheel, or
very sharp knife, and then slice into two equal rectangles, each
12 inches by 4 inches. Brush off any excess flour, and place the
rectangles in the refrigerator to chill while you make the filling.

To make the filling, place the almond paste and egg white in
a stand mixer fitted with the paddle attachment and beat until
well combined. Add the confectioners' sugar and cinnamon, and
beat to combine.

Remove one pastry dough rectangle from the refrigerator
and spread half of the filling down the center along the 12-inch
length. Roll the rectangle closed over the filling from one long
end to another, creating about a 12 x 1½-inch piece of dough.
Place it seam-side down, press gently to seal, then slice it into
6 pieces by cross-section, each 2 inches long. Cut 3 or 4 slits
halfway through the width of each individual pastry to create
toes, then spread the toes a bit out by bringing the edges of the
pastry toward one another to fan the pastry. Brush with the egg
wash, and place a slivered almond on each toe. Place each finished pastry on the prepared baking sheet, about 2 inches apart
from one another, then place in the freezer to chill until firm,
about 10 minutes. Repeat with the remaining pastry rectangle
and filling.

Place the baking sheet in the preheated oven and bake for
8 to 10 minutes, or until puffed and pale golden. Remove from
the oven and allow to cool on the baking sheet for about 10 minutes before serving.

one-bite apple fritters

MAKES ABOUT 20 FRITTERS

1 cup (140 g) all-purpose gluten-free flour (page 2)

1¼ teaspoons baking powder

3 tablespoons (36 g) granulated sugar

1 teaspoon ground cinnamon

½ teaspoon kosher salt

1 egg (50 g, weighed out of shell), at room temperature, beaten

½ cup (4 fluid ounces) milk, at room temperature

2 tablespoons (28 g) unsalted butter, melted and cooled

1 teaspoon pure vanilla extract

2 medium-size firm baking apples (Cortland or Granny Smith work well), peeled, cored, and cut into a ¼-inch dice (about 1½ cups diced apples)

Neutral oil, for frying

Confectioners' sugar for dusting

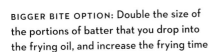

BIGGER BITE OPTION: Double the size of the portions of batter that you drop into the frying oil, and increase the frying time to about 5 minutes total per batch.

IF YOU'VE EVER SPENT THE DAY AT AN APPLE orchard during the season picking your own apples, gluten-filled fritters frying away, you know how hard it can be to endure that amazing smell and resist "cheating" on your gluten-free diet. The only cure for what ails you? Making your own fresh fritters with those very same apples fresh off the tree the moment you arrive home. May thoughts of these tender, fragrant bites of dough carry you through the day! Once fried, these fritters should be eaten right away.

In a large bowl, place the flour, baking powder, sugar, cinnamon, and salt, and whisk until well combined. Create a well in the center of the dry ingredients and add the egg, milk, butter, and vanilla, mixing to combine after each addition. Fold the diced apples into the batter.

Place paper towels on a plate, and set it aside. Place about 1 inch of oil in a medium-size, heavy-bottomed saucepan, and bring the oil to 360°F. Drop the fritter batter into the hot oil using a #70 or 1-tablespoon-size ice-cream scoop or two spoons in batches, taking care not to crowd the oil. Allow the fritters to fry, turning as necessary, until golden brown all over and cooked through, about 3 minutes total. Remove the cooked fritters from the oil with a slotted spoon or spider to the paper-towel-lined plate to drain. Bring the oil back to temperature between batches. Dust the warm fritters lightly with the confectioners' sugar and serve warm.

apple hand pies

APPLE PIE IS UNDENIABLY LOVELY. IT SMELLS LIKE A dream, and that classic combination of a light and flaky crust with fork-tender apples in a lightly sweet sauce is a hallmark of the fall season. So what could be better than that? Miniature apple pies, of course, where the ratio of crust to filling favors the filling, and the leftovers are easily frozen, then popped in the toaster oven like a grown-up toaster pastry.

Preheat your oven to 375°F. Line a large rimmed baking sheet with unbleached parchment paper and set it aside.

Make the biscuit dough according to the recipe instructions. Place the dough on a lightly floured surface, dust lightly with extra flour, and roll out until it is about ¼ inch thick. Cut out 2-inch rounds of dough from the pastry dough, then gather and reroll scraps. Dust the rounds very lightly with extra flour, stack them, and place in the refrigerator to chill.

Place the sliced apples in a large bowl, add the cinnamon, nutmeg, sugar, and salt, and toss to coat the apples evenly.

Remove the chilled crust from the freezer. Roll each round out so that it is closer to ⅛ inch thick and about 2½-inches round. You should have approximately 16 rounds. Using a pastry brush, brush the edges of half of the rounds with the egg wash. Place about 2 tablespoons of apple slices in the center of each prepared round, leaving a ¼-inch border around the edge. Top with the remaining rounds of dough, and cinch the edges together between your thumb and forefinger. Use the tines of a small fork to mark all around the perimeter of the assembled rounds to help seal them. Place the unbaked pies about 1 inch apart from one another on the prepared baking sheet, and place in the freezer until firm, about 10 minutes.

Remove the chilled pies from the oven, and use a very sharp knife to score the pies with two horizontal lines about 1 inch apart near the center of the top of each pie. Brush the tops of the pies generously with the egg wash. Cover the baking sheet with a sheet of aluminum foil, sealing it well around the edges of the baking sheet, but without allowing the foil to rest on the tops of the pies.

Place the pies in the center of the preheated oven, and bake for 15 minutes. Remove the foil, and bake until golden brown, about another 10 minutes. Serve warm.

MAKES 8 PIES

1 recipe Basic Pastry and Biscuit Dough (page 186)
2 large baking apples (Empire and Granny Smith work well), peeled, cored, and sliced thinly
1 teaspoon ground cinnamon
½ teaspoon freshly ground nutmeg
3 tablespoons sugar
Dash (⅛ teaspoon) kosher salt
Egg wash (1 egg beaten with 1 tablespoon milk), for brushing

⚜

MAKE-AHEAD OPTION: The pies can be filled and shaped, then frozen in a single layer on a baking sheet, before being piled into a freezer-safe bag and returned to the freezer. Bake from frozen, adding a few minutes on to the baking time.

BIGGER BITE OPTION: This recipe can also be used to make a traditional apple pie. Simply multiply the biscuit dough by 1½ and double the filling ingredients. Divide the pastry dough into two equal portions, and roll out each piece of dough into a 10-inch round. Place one round into a 9-inch pie plate, and press into the bottom and up the sides. Trim any excess dough. Assemble the filling ingredients, and place in the bottom crust. Place the second piecrust on top, trim the excess, and cinch the edges together. Score the top crust a few times with a sharp knife to allow steam to escape. Place the filled, raw pie in the freezer until firm, about 30 minutes. Cover the pie with two pieces of foil (top and bottom), and then place in the center of the preheated oven. Bake for 30 minutes. Remove the top piece of foil, brush the top crust with the egg wash, and return the pie to the oven. Continue to bake until golden brown all over, about another 30 minutes.

⚜

miniature vanilla bean scones

THERE'S A CERTAIN COFFEEHOUSE CHAIN THAT seems to have invaded the world, and it sells light, flaky, and petite vanilla bean scones that are juuuuust like these little gems. But since this isn't that cookbook, I'll leave the chain unnamed. Each of these miniature scones is gone in two to three bites, and they're just enough to satisfy with a steaming cup of dark, rich coffee. This recipe calls for Lyle's Golden Syrup, a liquid sweetener with a subtle buttery flavor. If you can't find Lyle's, try replacing it with light corn syrup. Honey is another possible alternative, but it has a much more prominent flavor than corn syrup or Lyle's.

Preheat your oven to 375°F. Line a rimmed baking sheet with unbleached parchment paper, and set it aside.

First, make the scones. In a large bowl, place the flour, nonfat dry milk, cornstarch, baking powder, baking soda, salt, and granulated sugar, and whisk to combine well. Add the chopped and chilled butter, and toss to coat it in the dry ingredients. Flatten each chunk of butter between your thumb and forefinger. Whisk the egg, seeds from half of a vanilla bean, Lyle's Golden Syrup (or light corn syrup or honey), and vanilla extract into the cream or milk. Create a well in the center of the dry ingredients, and add the cream or milk mixture. Mix gently until the dough begins to come together. If necessary, press together with floured hands, handling the dough as little as possible.

Turn out the dough onto a lightly floured piece of unbleached parchment paper, and press into a disk. Place another piece of unbleached parchment paper on top of the dough, and roll out into a rectangle that is about 1 inch thick. Remove the top piece of parchment paper, sprinkle lightly with flour, and fold the dough over on itself like you would a business letter. Sprinkle the dough again lightly with flour, replace the parchment paper, and roll out the dough once again into a rectangle about 1 inch thick. Once more, remove the top piece of parchment paper, sprinkle lightly with flour, and fold the dough over on itself like you would a business letter. Sprinkle the dough again lightly with flour, replace the parchment paper, and roll out the dough, but this time roll into a 7-inch square that is about ¾ inch thick. The dough should have a smooth, even

MAKES 16 SCONES

FOR THE SCONES

- 1½ cups plus 2 tablespoons (227 g) all-purpose gluten-free flour (page 2), plus more for sprinkling
- 5 tablespoons (30 g) nonfat dry milk, ground to a fine powder in a blender or food processor
- 3 tablespoons (27 g) cornstarch
- 1½ teaspoons baking powder
- ¼ teaspoon baking soda
- ½ teaspoon kosher salt
- ¼ cup (50 g) granulated sugar
- 5 tablespoons (70 g) unsalted butter, chopped and chilled
- 1 egg (60 g, out of shell), beaten and chilled
- Seeds from ½ vanilla bean
- 2 tablespoons (42 g) Lyle's Golden Syrup, light corn syrup, or honey
- 1 tablespoon pure vanilla extract
- ⅔ cup (5⅓ fluid ounces) heavy whipping cream, chilled (can use milk instead—just not nonfat)

FOR THE VANILLA BEAN GLAZE

- Seeds from ½ a vanilla bean
- 1½ cups (173 g) confectioners' sugar
- 2 tablespoons milk (any kind), plus more by the ¼ teaspoonful, as necessary

---
‧ ⚘ ‧

MAKE-AHEAD OPTION: These pastries can be made and shaped, then frozen raw in a single layer on a baking sheet before being piled in a freezer-safe zip-top bag and returned to the freezer. They can be baked right from frozen and finished by following the recipe directions; simply add a few minutes to the baking time. They can also be shaped and refrigerated in a covered single layer for up to 3 days before baking. Once baked, they are best eaten the same day.

BIGGER BITE OPTION: Rather than cutting each of the 4 original squares of dough into 4 triangles, cut them diagonally through the center into 2 triangles. Increase the baking time by about 4 minutes.

‧ ⚘ ‧
---

surface. Peel back the top piece of parchment paper, and with a sharp knife or bench or bowl scraper, cut the dough into 4 equal squares. Cut each square into 4 equal triangles by cutting an X through the center of the square. Place the wedges about 2 inches apart from one another on the prepared baking sheet, and chill in the freezer until firm, about 10 minutes.

Remove the baking sheet from the freezer and place in the center of the preheated oven. Bake until the scones are puffed and very pale golden, about 10 minutes. Remove from the oven and allow to cool for 10 minutes on the baking sheet before transferring to a wire rack to cool completely.

While the scones are cooling, make the glaze. In a small bowl, mix the seeds from the (other) half of the vanilla bean into the confectioners' sugar until the seeds are evenly distributed throughout the sugar. Add 2 tablespoons of milk, and mix well, until a thick paste forms. Add more milk by the ¼ teaspoon, mixing to combine well, until the glaze falls off the spoon slowly, in a thick but pourable glaze. Add milk very slowly, as it is much easier to thin, than to thicken, the glaze. If you do thin the glaze too much, add more confectioners' sugar a teaspoon at a time to thicken it. Either dip the tops of the cooled scones into the glaze, or spoon it on top of the scones and spread into an even layer. Allow to set at room temperature before serving.

miniature chocolate éclairs

LIKE THEIR SAVORY COUSINS, THE CHEESE PUFFS *(page 28), these miniature chocolate éclairs are deceptively easy to make. If you're in a rush or are trying this recipe for the first time and planning to serve it to guests and are concerned about getting it just right, replace the pastry cream either with boxed vanilla pudding or even just whipped cream. Everyone will be so dazzled by the delicate pastry shell and chocolate topping that they'll never know. Note that you'll need a small Bismarck pastry tube tip for filling the éclairs (I use the Ateco 230 tip, but any small tip will do).*

First, make the pastries. Preheat your oven to 375°F. Line two large rimmed baking sheets with unbleached parchment paper, and set them aside. Heat the milk, butter, and salt in a medium-size, heavy-bottomed saucepan over medium heat until the butter is completely melted and the mixture begins to simmer, about 4 minutes. Remove the pan from the heat, and add the flour, stirring vigorously until the mixture comes together. Return the pan to the heat and cook, stirring vigorously, until the mixture begins to pull away from the sides of the pan and comes together in a ball, about 2 minutes. A thin film will form on the bottom of the pan. Remove from the heat, and allow the mixture to cool for at least 3 minutes, or until it is no longer hot to the touch.

Transfer half the cooled dough to a blender or food processor. Pour the beaten eggs on top and then add the rest of the dough. Pulse until the mixture is smooth and uniformly well blended. Transfer the pastry dough to a pastry bag fitted with a large, plain piping tip (about 1 inch in diameter). Pipe the dough into portions about 1 inch wide and 3 inches long onto the prepared baking sheets, each portion about 2 inches apart from one another. Smooth the tops of the pastry dough lightly with wet fingers so that nothing will burn during baking. Bake the pastry in the center of the preheated oven for 18 to 20 minutes, or until puffed and pale golden. Remove the baking sheets from the oven, and working quickly, with a sharp knife, cut a small slit in the side of each pastry to allow steam to escape. Return the pastries on the baking sheets to the oven, turn off the oven,

FOR THE CHOUX PASTRY

1 cup (8 fluid ounces) milk (not nonfat)
4 tablespoons (56 g) unsalted butter, at room temperature
1/8 teaspoon kosher salt
1 cup (140 g) Gluten-Free Pastry Flour (page 5)
4 eggs (200 g, weighed out of shell), at room temperature, beaten

FOR THE PASTRY CREAM

2 cups (16 fluid ounces) milk, divided
1/2 cup (100 g) granulated sugar
1/4 teaspoon kosher salt
4 egg yolks (100 g), at room temperature
1/4 cup (35 g) Basic Gum-Free Gluten-Free Flour (page 4)
1 teaspoon pure vanilla extract
Seeds from 1/2 vanilla bean (optional)

FOR THE CHOCOLATE TOPPING

4 ounces dark chocolate, chopped
2 tablespoons (24 g) vegetable shortening (or virgin coconut oil)

and prop open the oven door slightly. Allow them to sit in the oven until dry, about 30 minutes. Once the éclairs are dry, prepare to fill them.

To make the pastry cream, in a medium-size, heavy-bottomed saucepan, place 1¾ cups of the milk, sugar, and salt, and whisk to combine. Bring the mixture to a simmer over medium-low heat. While the milk is coming to a simmer, in a separate medium, heat-safe bowl, mix together the egg yolks, remaining ¼ cup of milk, and the flour until smooth. Once the milk and sugar mixture has come to a simmer, remove from the heat and drizzle the hot milk very slowly into the egg yolk mixture, whisking constantly. Once the milk has all been added to the egg yolk mixture, transfer the whole mixture back to the saucepan and cook over medium-low heat, whisking constantly, until the pastry cream has begun to bubble and thicken, about 1 minute. Remove the saucepan from the heat, and whisk in the vanilla extract and (optional) vanilla seeds. Strain the pastry cream through a fine-mesh sieve into a medium-size bowl to remove any lumps. Continue to whisk the pastry cream until it is no longer hot to the touch. Place plastic wrap directly on the surface of the pastry cream, and refrigerate until firm (at least 30 minutes, but up to 3 days).

Remove the pastry cream from the refrigerator, remove the plastic wrap, and transfer the cream to a pastry bag fitted with a small Bismarck pastry tube or other small tip. Pierce the first éclair with the pastry tip and pipe the filling inside. Repeat with the remaining éclairs.

To make the chocolate topping, place the chopped chocolate and shortening in a medium-size, heat-safe bowl, and melt either in short 30-second bursts in the microwave or over a simmering pot of water in a double boiler. Allow the chocolate to cool briefly before pouring the chocolate topping over each filled éclair, spreading it evenly over the top. Allow to sit at room temperature until the chocolate has set.

MAKE-AHEAD OPTION: The pastry cream can be made and stored in a sealed container in the refrigerator for up to 3 days. The pastry dough may be made ahead of time, placed in a sealed container, and stored in the refrigerator for up to 5 days. Allow the dough to come to room temperature before piping and baking as directed. Once fully prepared, these are best eaten right away.

BIGGER BITE OPTION: Make full-size chocolate éclairs by piping the dough with a 1½-inch plain piping tip in portions that are 4½ inches long by 1½ inches wide. Increase the baking time to about 25 minutes, depending upon size.

miniature cannoli

MAKES 20 CANNOLI

FOR THE SHELLS

2 cups (280 g) all-purpose gluten-free flour (page 2)

¼ cup (30 g) confectioners' sugar

1 teaspoon ground cinnamon

¼ teaspoon kosher salt

¾ cup (6 fluid ounces) Marsala wine, at room temperature (see note)

3 tablespoons (42 g) unsalted butter, at room temperature

Lukewarm water by the ½ teaspoonful, as necessary

Neutral oil, for frying

Egg wash (1 egg beaten with 1 tablespoon water)

Note: To replace Marsala wine, use 10 tablespoons dry white wine (like pinot grigio) plus 2 tablespoons brandy, or 10 tablespoons white grape juice plus 2 table-spoons sherry vinegar for an alcohol-free option.

FOR THE FILLING

1½ cups (336 g) ricotta cheese, at room temperature

12 ounces mascarpone cheese, at room temperature

½ cup (100 g) granulated sugar

1 teaspoon pure vanilla extract

¼ teaspoon kosher salt

¼ cup (2 fluid ounces) heavy whipping cream, chilled

3 ounces miniature chocolate chips

MOST COOKS WOULD NOT EVEN CONSIDER MAKING these at home. But if we want to have an authentic gluten-free cannoli, we're going to have to make it ourselves because there really aren't good packaged options out there. If the only thing keeping you from trying your hand at cannoli is not having cannoli forms, those small hollow aluminum cylinders around which you wrap the raw shell to create the proper shape during frying, try using a large wooden clothespin or, better yet, a wooden dowel wrapped tightly in aluminum foil instead. If you've gotta have cannoli, you've gotta have it!

First, make the shells. In a large bowl, place the flour, confectioners' sugar, cinnamon, and salt, and whisk to combine well. Create a well in the center of the dry ingredients, and add the wine and butter, mixing to combine after each addition. The dough should come together and be thick and stiff but not unworkable. If it seems too stiff to shape, add water by the ½ teaspoonful, kneading it into the dough until you reach the proper consistency. Place the dough on a lightly floured surface, and roll out ¼ inch thick, sprinkling very lightly with extra flour and moving the dough around as necessary to prevent sticking. Using a 3-inch round cookie cutter, cut out rounds of dough. Sprinkle the rounds very lightly with extra flour, and roll out until the rounds are ⅛ inch thick and 4 inches in diameter. Gather and reroll scraps until the dough has all been used.

Place about 3 inches of oil in a large, heavy-bottomed pan, and bring the oil to 360°F over medium-high heat. Spray the cannoli forms with cooking oil spray to prevent sticking. One at a time, begin to wrap one piece of shaped dough around one form, brushing the dough lightly with egg wash to help the dough stick to itself where it overlaps. Set the form aside and repeat with the remaining forms and pieces of dough. Lower the forms wrapped in the dough into the frying oil by placing a few at a time in the frying basket or spider/wok strainer. Allow the shells to fry until lightly golden brown all over, turning over gently halfway through to ensure even browning, about 5 minutes total. Remove the shells, still on the forms, from the frying oil with tongs, and place on a wire rack positioned above paper towels to drain and crisp. Bring the oil back to temperature between batches.

Make the filling while the shells are cooling. In a medium-size bowl, place the ricotta cheese, mascarpone cheese, sugar, vanilla, and salt, and whisk to combine well. Add the heavy whipping cream to the bowl and beat with a handheld mixer (or very vigorously with a handheld whisk), until the filling begins to thicken slightly. Fold in the miniature chocolate chips, and place the filling in the refrigerator to chill for about 10 minutes. Place the filling in a piping bag fitted with a medium-size open piping tip. Remove the cooled shells from the forms, and pipe the filling into the cooled shells from both sides until it meets in the middle. Serve immediately.

cheesecake bites

EVERYONE'S FAVORITE CLASSIC CHEESECAKE IS JUST more fun when in miniature form. For a touch of chocolate, try adding a few mini chocolate chips to the filling right before baking. The miniature cheesecakes are placed in a water bath to ensure even, gentle baking with no cracks. I like the crusts best when they're made with crushed Snickerdoodle Cookie Chips (page 154), but either of the other cookie chips (see pages 152–155) would work perfectly well.

Preheat your oven to 325°F. Line a 24-cup muffin tin, and set it aside. In this recipe, the wells of the muffin tin must be lined, not greased, or the cheesecakes won't hold together properly.

In a medium-size bowl, place the cookie crumbs, melted butter, and egg white, and mix until all crumbs are moistened. Place about 1 teaspoon of the cookie crumb mixture in each of the prepared wells of the muffin tin, and press firmly into an even layer on the bottom and very slightly up the sides. Set aside.

Make the cheesecake batter. In the bowl of your stand mixer fitted with the paddle attachment (or in a bowl with a hand mixer), beat the softened cream cheese on medium-high speed until it is light and fluffy. Add the sugar, eggs, vanilla, and salt, beating on medium-high speed after each addition until smooth. With a spring-loaded ice-cream scoop, fill each well of the miniature muffin tin about three-quarters of the way full with the cheesecake batter. Shake the pan from side to side to distribute the cheesecake in an even layer. Place a large baking dish with at least 4-inch sides, into which your muffin tin can rest, in the center of the preheated oven. With the oven rack pulled halfway out of the oven, fill the large pan halfway with water (or high enough that the water will come at least halfway up the undersides of the wells of the muffin tin). Rest the muffin tin on top of the water bath in the large pan, carefully slide in the rack, and close the oven.

Bake, without opening the oven, for about 20 minutes or until the cheesecakes are just set. To prevent the cheesecakes from cracking as they cool, turn the oven off, and allow the cheesecakes to sit in the oven with the door ajar until the oven temperature cools to about 200°F. Place the muffin tin on a wire rack to allow the cheesecakes to cool for 10 minutes before removing from the muffin wells and placing directly on the rack to cool completely. Repeat with the remaining ingredients.

MAKES ABOUT 30 BITES

FOR THE CRUST
1 cup gluten-free cookie crumbs (like the Snickerdoodle Cookie Chips, page 154, crushed)
4 tablespoons (56 g) butter, melted
1 egg white (25 g), at room temperature

FOR THE CHEESECAKE FILLING
2 8-ounce packages cream cheese, at room temperature
1 cup (200 g) granulated sugar
2 eggs (100 g, weighed out of shell) at room temperature, beaten
1 teaspoon pure vanilla extract
¼ teaspoon kosher salt

———————— ⚓ ————————

MAKE-AHEAD OPTION: These cheesecake bites can be made ahead of time, cooled completely, and then stored in a single layer in a sealed container in the refrigerator for up to 5 days.

BIGGER BITE OPTION: This same recipe can be made into a single 9-inch round cheesecake. Follow the directions as written, but press the crust into a greased 9-inch springform pan, and then pour in the filling. Wrap the bottom of the pan tightly in foil, then place the cheesecake in a water bath, and bake as directed, increasing the baking time to about 35 minutes. Allow to cool slowly in the oven in the same manner.

———————— ⚓ ————————

petit fours

THESE SMALL AND DELICATE ALMOND-FLAVORED confections *are sweetened with a coating of pourable fondant. Very similar in taste and texture to the tricolor rainbow cookies you find in Italian bakeries, right down to the jam in between the layers, these delicate little cakes are a favorite of almond lovers—and little girls making tea parties—everywhere.*

MAKES ABOUT 45 CONFECTIONS

FOR THE CAKES

8 ounces gluten-free almond paste, broken up into small pieces

16 tablespoons (224 g) unsalted butter, at room temperature

¾ cup (150 g) granulated sugar

¼ teaspoon kosher salt

4 eggs (200 g, weighed out of shell), at room temperature, beaten

2 cups (280 g) all-purpose gluten-free flour (page 2)

½ cup seedless raspberry or strawberry jam, heated slightly to make spreadable

FOR THE POURABLE FONDANT

5 ounces white chocolate, chopped

1 cup (115 g) confectioners' sugar

¼ cup (84 g) light corn syrup

1 teaspoon pure vanilla extract

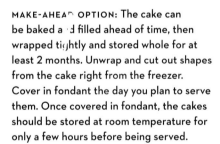

MAKE-AHEAD OPTION: The cake can be baked and filled ahead of time, then wrapped tightly and stored whole for at least 2 months. Unwrap and cut out shapes from the cake right from the freezer. Cover in fondant the day you plan to serve them. Once covered in fondant, the cakes should be stored at room temperature for only a few hours before being served.

BIGGER BITE OPTION: Rather than cutting the cake into small squares, cut it into larger shapes, or just serve as a simple two-layer cake. It's delicious enough to stand on its own, no fondant needed!

Preheat your oven to 350°F. Line 2 quarter sheet pans (each 12 inches by 9 inches) with unbleached parchment paper, and set them aside.

In the bowl of a stand mixer fitted with the paddle attachment (or a large bowl with a hand mixer), cream the almond paste and butter until well combined. Add the sugar, salt, and eggs, beating to combine well after each addition. The batter should be thick. Add the flour, and mix until the dough is smooth. Divide into 2 equal parts (each about 750 grams), and stretch and press into an even layer in each pan, using wet fingers and a wet spatula. The dough will be sticky.

Place each pan, one at a time, in the center of the preheated oven, and bake for about 12 minutes, or until the dough just begins to brown around the edges. Remove the pan from the oven and allow to cool slightly. Invert one slightly cooled cake onto a large piece of parchment paper, and evenly spread the jam on it. Invert the second layer carefully on top, taking care not to handle the cakes too much or they may begin to crack. Place a sheet of parchment paper on top, and place a heavy book on top of the stack to compress the layers. Place the stack of cakes, along with the book perched on top, in the refrigerator for about 30 minutes, or until the layers have begun to flatten and compress. Cut the compressed cake into 1½-inch squares with a sharp knife or square cookie cutter.

Place a wire rack over a parchment-lined sheet pan, and set it aside. In a medium-size, heat-safe bowl, melt the white chocolate in the microwave in 30-second bursts at 60% power, stirring in between, or place the bowl over a small pot of gently simmering water making sure the water doesn't touch the bowl, until the chocolate is melted. Remove the bowl from the heat, then add the confectioners' sugar, corn syrup, and vanilla, stirring to combine after each addition. The fondant should be thickly pourable. Spoon over the cooled cakes, and allow to set at room temperature.

chapter 8: breads, tortillas
& doughs

basic pastry and biscuit dough

MAKES 1³/₄ POUNDS

2½ cups (350 g) Gluten-Free Pastry Flour (page 5), plus more for sprinkling

4 teaspoons baking powder

¾ teaspoon baking soda

1¼ teaspoons (8 g) kosher salt

10 tablespoons (140 g) unsalted butter, cut into large chunks and chilled

1¼ cups (10 fluid ounces) milk or cream (not nonfat)

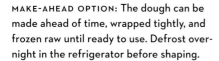

MAKE-AHEAD OPTION: The dough can be made ahead of time, wrapped tightly, and frozen raw until ready to use. Defrost overnight in the refrigerator before shaping.

THIS RECIPE FOR BASIC PASTRY DOUGH IS LIKE THE engine that drives so many of the recipes in this cookbook. It's laminated a bit, which is just a fancy word for alternating layers of butter and dough in pastry, which is what leads to flakiness in the oven. It may require a few minutes more effort than a typical piecrust, but the effort pays off in spades when you see and taste the many layers of pastry. Rather than fussing with a million different types of pastry crust, this is the only pastry recipe you'll really need—even for empanadas, if you choose.

In a large bowl, place the flour, baking powder, baking soda, and salt, and whisk to combine well. Add the chopped butter to the flour mixture, and toss to coat. Place each piece of butter between your floured thumb and index finger to flatten it until it's about ¼ inch thick. Create a well in the center of the flour mixture, and pour in the milk or cream. Mix with a large spoon or spatula until the dough begins to come together.

Turn the dough out onto a lightly floured surface, dust it lightly with more flour, and roll out the dough with a rolling pin into a thick rectangle. It will be shaggy and not smooth. Fold the rectangle in half lengthwise, dust again lightly with flour, and roll the dough out again into a thick rectangle. Once more, fold the rectangle in half lengthwise, and then fold again widthwise to create a much smaller, thicker rectangle. The dough should have begun to take on a smoother appearance. Brush off any surface excess flour and transfer the folded dough to a large piece of plastic wrap and wrap tightly.

Serving and storage: Place the dough in the refrigerator to chill for at least an hour and up to 5 days before using according to the instructions for the recipe you have selected. For longer storage, wrap the pastry dough tightly in freezer-safe wrap and freeze. Defrost overnight in the refrigerator before following recipe instructions for its use.

rich savory pastry crust

MAKES ABOUT 1 POUND
OF DOUGH

1¾ cups (245 g) Gluten-Free Pastry Flour
(page 5)

½ teaspoon kosher salt

8 tablespoons (112 g) unsalted butter,
roughly chopped and chilled

1 egg yolk (25 g)

½ cup (4 fluid ounces) water, iced (ice
doesn't count in volume measurement)

—————————— ⚘ ——————————

MAKE-AHEAD OPTION: The dough can be
made ahead of time, wrapped tightly, and
frozen raw until ready to use. Defrost overnight in the refrigerator before shaping.

—————————— ⚘ ——————————

THE MAIN DIFFERENCES BETWEEN THIS PASTRY CRUST
and the Basic Pastry and Biscuit Dough (page 186), other than
the proportions of ingredients, are that this recipe has no chem-
ical leaveners (the biscuit dough has both baking powder and
baking soda), and it calls for one egg yolk to be beaten into
the ice water that brings the dough together. The result is a
smoother, slightly less flaky, richer dough that is perfect for
quiches (see pages 117, 118).

In a large bowl, place the flour and salt, and whisk to combine
well. Add the chopped and chilled butter, and toss to coat the
butter in the dry ingredients. Press each floured chunk of butter
between a floured thumb and forefinger to flatten. In a small
bowl, whisk the egg yolk and ½ cup water until well combined.
Create a well in the center of the large bowl of dry ingredients,
add the egg yolk and water mixture, and mix to combine. The
dough will come together. If there are any very crumbly bits,
add more ice water by the tablespoon and mix to combine.

Turn the dough out onto a lightly floured surface, dust it
lightly with more flour, and roll out the dough with a rolling pin
into a thick rectangle. It will be shaggy and not smooth. Fold the
rectangle in half lengthwise, dust again lightly with flour, and
roll the dough out again into a thick rectangle. Once more, fold
the rectangle in half lengthwise, and then fold again widthwise
to create a much smaller, thicker rectangle. The dough should
have begun to take on a smoother appearance. Brush off any
surface excess flour, transfer the folded dough to a large piece
of plastic wrap, and wrap tightly.

Serving and storage: Place the dough in the refrigerator to
chill for at least an hour and up to 5 days before using according to the instructions for the recipe you have selected. For
longer storage, wrap the pastry dough tightly in freezer-safe
wrap and freeze. Defrost overnight in the refrigerator before
following recipe instructions for its use.

empanada dough

EMPANADA DOUGH IS A FORM OF PASTRY DOUGH, SO it should be kept as cold as possible during handling. It has a distinct depth of flavor that our Basic Pastry and Biscuit Dough (page 186) doesn't have, of course, as the recipe calls for both a dry white wine and for eggs, and is made with a mix of butter and shortening. If you prefer to use all shortening, just replace the butter 1:1, but you may need a touch more liquid. Likewise with replacing the shortening with butter, but in that case you may need a touch less liquid.

In a large bowl, place the pastry flour and salt and whisk to combine well. Add the chopped butter and chopped shortening, and toss to coat the pieces in the flour mixture. Place each piece of butter and shortening between your floured thumb and index finger to flatten it until it's about ¼ inch thick. In a separate small bowl or measuring cup with a pour spout, place the white wine, cider vinegar, and eggs, and whisk to combine well. Create a well in the center of the dry ingredients, add the white wine mixture, and mix until the dough begins to come together. Add more flour by the teaspoonful as necessary to bring the dough together without its being too moist. Turn the dough out onto a large piece of plastic wrap, cover the dough, and press gently into a disk. Place in the refrigerator to chill, wrapped tightly in plastic wrap, for about 30 minutes.

Turn the chilled dough out onto a lightly floured surface, sprinkle with extra flour, and roll it out into a rectangle that is about 1 inch thick, moving the dough frequently and sprinkling lightly with more flour as necessary to prevent any sticking. Sprinkle the top of the dough lightly with flour, and fold it over on itself like you would a business letter. Sprinkle again lightly with flour, roll out the dough once again into a rectangle about 1 inch thick, sprinkle lightly again with flour, and fold the dough over on itself once more like you would a business letter. Repeat the process at least once more until you have a smooth dough that rolls out easily before finally rolling the dough into a rectangle a bit less than ¼ inch thick. Using a 3-inch round biscuit or cookie cutter, cut out rounds of dough. Sprinkle each round lightly with more flour, roll out into a 4-inch round, then gather

MAKES ABOUT 25 4-INCH
ROUNDS OF DOUGH

3 cups (420 g) Gluten-Free Pastry Flour (page 5), plus more as necessary

1½ teaspoons kosher salt

6 tablespoons (84 g) unsalted butter, roughly chopped and chilled

7 tablespoons (84 g) nonhydrogenated vegetable shortening, chopped

⅓ cup (2⅔ fluid ounces) dry white wine (like pinot grigio), chilled (see note)

2 teaspoons apple cider vinegar

2 eggs (100 g, weighed out of shell), beaten

Note: To replace the wine with an alcohol-free substitute, try equal parts white grape juice plus sherry vinegar.

and reroll scraps until most of the dough has been cut into rounds, rolling each out into a 4-inch round as you go.

Serving and storage: Stack the rounds, then cover them tightly with plastic wrap and store in the refrigerator until you are ready to use them. For longer storage, wrap tightly in freezer-safe wrap and freeze. Defrost overnight in the refrigerator before following recipe instructions for their use.

———————✿———————

MAKE-AHEAD OPTION: The dough can be made ahead of time, shaped and stacked with a light dusting of flour between rounds, wrapped tightly, and frozen raw until ready to use. Defrost slightly before using so that the pastry doesn't crack when you try to shape it.

BIGGER BITE OPTION: The dough can be rolled out and cut into whatever shapes and sizes you like.

———————✿———————

wonton wrappers

WONTON WRAPPERS ARE ANOTHER ONE OF THOSE super simple doughs (flours, egg, and water are all it takes) that power so many of the best recipes in this cookbook. Gluten eaters can just wander into a well-stocked grocery store and pull a package of wonton wrappers off the shelf and make anything from egg rolls and pot stickers to Baked Pork Spring Rolls in the blink of an eye. While we dream of the day that really good gluten-free wonton wrappers are available for purchase, let's make our own. They freeze beautifully, so make a big batch.

MAKES 60 3-INCH-SQUARE WRAPPERS

1¾ cups (245 g) all-purpose gluten-free flour (page 2), plus more for sprinkling

35 grams (about ¼ cup) Expandex modified tapioca starch (page 3) (can be replaced with an equal amount of plain tapioca starch/flour)

3 eggs (150 g, weighed out of shell), at room temperature, beaten

4 to 6 tablespoons warm water (about 85°F)

In the bowl of a stand mixer fitted with the paddle attachment (or a large bowl with a wooden spoon), place the flour and Expandex, and whisk to combine well with a separate handheld whisk. Create a well in the center of the dry ingredients, add the eggs and 4 tablespoons warm water, and mix to combine on medium speed for about 1 minute. The dough should come together. If there are any crumbly bits, add the remaining warm water by the teaspoonful until the dough holds together well when squeezed with your hands. Turn the mixer speed up to medium high, and beat until smooth, 3 to 4 minutes. The dough should be smooth and pliable. If it feels stiff, add a few more drops of water and mix in until pliable. It should be, at most, slightly sticky but mostly just smooth.

Transfer the dough to a piece of plastic wrap, wrap it tightly, and allow it to sit at room temperature for about 10 minutes. The dough will absorb more water and any remaining stickiness should dissipate. Unwrap the dough, and divide it in half. Return half of it to the plastic wrap, and wrap tightly to prevent it from drying out. Place the remaining half of the dough on a lightly floured surface, sprinkle lightly with more flour, and roll into a rectangle about ¼ inch thick. Flip and shift the dough often to prevent it from sticking, sprinkling very lightly with more flour as necessary to allow movement. With a pizza wheel, pastry cutter, or sharp knife, trim the edges of the rectangle to create even edges. Remove and gather the trimmings, and set them aside.

Using even and sustained pressure, roll out the rectangle until it is approximately ⅛ inch thick. Slice into 3-inch squares. Alternatively, slice the ¼-inch-thick rectangle into 1½-inch squares, and roll each square evenly in all directions until it

doubles in surface area and is ⅛ inch thick. I often find this the quicker, easier way to get squares that are the proper thickness. Proceed with the recipe instructions for using the wrappers.

Serving and storage: The wonton wrappers may be covered with a moist tea towel and kept at room temperature for about 2 hours until you are ready to serve them. They can also be dusted lightly with flour and stacked, then wrapped tightly in freezer-safe wrap and frozen. Defrost in the refrigerator before proceeding with the instructions in the recipe you are following for use of the dough.

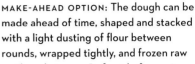

MAKE-AHEAD OPTION: The dough can be made ahead of time, shaped and stacked with a light dusting of flour between rounds, wrapped tightly, and frozen raw until ready to use. Defrost before using so that the rounds are pliable enough to shape.

BIGGER BITE OPTION: The dough can be rolled out and cut into whatever shapes and sizes you like, including larger shapes as for the Egg Rolls on page 35.

phyllo dough

MAKES ABOUT 15 10 X 8-INCH
SHEETS

3½ cups (490 g) all-purpose gluten-free
flour (page 2)

¾ cup (85 g) Expandex modified tapioca
starch (page 3) (can be replaced with
an equal amount of plain tapioca starch/
flour)

1 teaspoon kosher salt

¼ cup (56 g) extra-virgin olive oil

3 tablespoons freshly squeezed lemon
juice

1½ cups (12 fluid ounces) lukewarm water

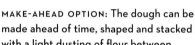

MAKE-AHEAD OPTION: The dough can be
made ahead of time, shaped and stacked
with a light dusting of flour between
layers, then placed in the freezer, flat on
a baking sheet, unwrapped and raw, until
frozen solid. Once frozen, wrap the layers
tightly but handle the dough gently so it
doesn't break. Return to the freezer until
ready to use. It will defrost very quickly at
room temperature.

BEFORE YOU TURN THE PAGE, ROLLING YOUR EYES that I would even suggest that you make your own phyllo dough, hear me out. If you ever (and I do mean ever) want to have authentic gluten-free Greek spanakopita, you will have to make your own phyllo (or at least talk someone else into doing it for you). After you realize that, you'll be willing to trust me that it's no harder than rolling out piecrust or tortillas, as long as you have the right recipe (right here!) and you're willing to roll, roll, roll, and then roll some more. Think of it this way: it's a great time to catch up on your podcasts!

In a large bowl, place the flour, Expandex, and salt, and whisk to combine. Create a well in the center of the dry ingredients, add the olive oil, lemon juice, and water, and mix to combine. The dough will come together and be thick. Press together into a ball, cover with a moist tea towel, and allow to sit for about 20 minutes. The dough will stiffen a bit as it absorbs more of the water.

Pull off golf-ball-size pieces (about 3 ounces by weight) of the dough, and press into a disk with your fingers. Place the dough on a clean, flat surface and roll into a rough rectangle about 8 inches long. Sprinkle lightly with flour, and roll into a rectangle about 12 inches by 10 inches. Using a sharp knife, pizza wheel, or pastry cutter, trim the rough edges of the rectangle into a neat rectangle that is about 10 inches by 8 inches. Dust both sides of the dough generously with more flour, and set aside on a piece of parchment paper. Gather the scraps and return them to the remaining dough. Repeat with the rest of the dough, layering the pieces of rolled-out dough on top of one another, each dusted generously with flour to prevent sticking. Proceed with the recipe instructions for using the phyllo dough.

Serving and storage: Fresh phyllo sheets can be covered with a moist tea towel for about 2 hours until you are ready to use them. The sheets can also be cooled completely in a stack, placed flat on a baking sheet and frozen solid, then wrapped tightly in freezer-safe wrap and returned to the freezer until ready to use. Defrost in the refrigerator before proceeding with the instructions in the recipe you are following for use of the dough.

crêpes

THIN, DELICATE FRENCH PANCAKES, CRÊPES ARE incredibly easy to make and very pliable. Don't let those lacy edges fool you; they're also surprisingly sturdy. More savory than flour tortillas, particularly because of the eggs in the batter, they are not a perfect substitute for flour tortillas but can be used in a pinch.

In a large bowl, place the flour and salt, and whisk to combine well. In a separate, small bowl, place the eggs, butter, and milk, and whisk to combine well. Create a well in the center of the flour and pour in the wet ingredients. Whisk until very well combined. The batter will thicken a bit as you whisk.

For best results, cover the bowl and place the batter in the refrigerator overnight or for up to 2 days. Before using the batter, remove it from the refrigerator, whisk until smooth, and allow it come to room temperature. The batter should be about the consistency of half-and-half (thicker than milk, thinner than heavy cream). Transfer the batter to a large spouted measuring cup.

Heat a heavy-bottomed nonstick 9-inch skillet (or a well-seasoned and lightly greased 9-inch cast-iron skillet) over medium heat for 2 minutes. Holding the warm skillet just above the flame, carefully pour about 5 tablespoons (a bit more than ¼ cup) of batter right into the center of the skillet, and swirl the pan to distribute the batter evenly across the entire flat surface of the pan. Once you get a rhythm going, you should be able to begin swirling as soon as the first drop of batter hits the pan. Cook over medium heat until the edges and underside of the crêpe are lightly golden brown, about 90 seconds. With a wide spatula (and/or your fingers, carefully), turn the crêpe over and cook until the other side is lightly golden brown, about another 45 seconds. Slide the crêpe out of the skillet onto a parchment-lined plate. Repeat with the remaining batter, stacking the finished crêpes on top of one another.

Serving and storage: The crêpes may be covered with a moist tea towel and kept at room temperature for about 2 hours until you are ready to serve them. They can also be cooled completely in a stack, then wrapped tightly in freezer-safe wrap and frozen. Defrost at room temperature and refresh by placing on a hot, dry skillet for about 30 seconds per side.

MAKES ABOUT 12 CRÊPES

1¾ cups (245 g) Basic Gum-Free Gluten-Free Flour (page 4)

¼ teaspoon kosher salt

3 eggs (150 g, weighed out of shell) at room temperature, beaten

2 tablespoons (28 g) unsalted butter, melted and cooled

2 cups (16 fluid ounces) milk, at room temperature

MAKE-AHEAD OPTION: Crêpes can be made ahead of time, shaped and cooked, then stacked on top of one another and frozen on a baking sheet unwrapped. Then, wrap them tightly and freeze until ready to use. Defrost at room temperature completely, then refresh in a hot, dry skillet, about 30 seconds per side. Once the crêpes are completely defrosted, they should be easy to separate from one another. The crêpe batter can be made and stored in a sealed container in the refrigerator for up to 3 days, provided your ingredients are fresh. Bring the batter to room temperature before cooking with it.

flour tortillas

MAKES ABOUT 12 8-INCH TORTILLAS

1¾ cups (245 g) all-purpose gluten-free flour (page 2), plus more for sprinkling

¼ cup (35 g) Expandex modified tapioca starch (page 3) (can be replaced with an equal amount of plain tapioca starch/flour)

1½ teaspoons baking powder

1 teaspoon (6 g) kosher salt

4½ tablespoons (54 g) vegetable shortening

¾ cup (6 ounces) warm water (about 85°F)

EVER SINCE I DEVELOPED THIS, THE PERFECT RECIPE for gluten-free flour tortillas, for Gluten-Free on a Shoestring Bakes Bread, it has been on constant rotation in my house—and at least one batch has a perpetual spot in my freezer. Whenever I'm not sure what to make for dinner, I turn to flour tortillas. They truly bend without breaking when they're fresh or have been refreshed in a skillet, even after they've spent the better part of two months in the deep freeze. I just can't seem to make it through the week without these versatile beauties. Although an 8-inch cake cutter is ideal for cutting out clean tortilla circles, a similarly sized pot lid with a well-defined edge works quite well.

In a large bowl, place the flour, Expandex, baking powder, and salt, and whisk to combine. Add the vegetable shortening, and toss it in the dry ingredients. With the tines of a large fork, break up the shortening into small pieces about the size of small peas. Create a well in the center of the mixture, and add the water. Mix to combine. The dough will come together and be thick. Press together into a ball, cover with a moist tea towel, and allow to sit for about 20 minutes. The dough will stiffen a bit as it absorbs more of the water.

Heat a 10- or 12-inch cast-iron skillet over medium-high heat. Divide the dough into about 8 pieces. Begin with one piece of dough, and cover the rest with a moist tea towel to prevent them from drying out. On a lightly floured surface, with a rolling pin, roll out the first piece of dough until it is about ⅛ inch thick. Cut out a round with an 8-inch metal cake cutter or a similarly sized lid of a pot. Stack the raw tortillas on top of one another, dusting lightly with flour between them, if necessary, to prevent them from sticking. Gather the scraps and set them aside. Repeat with the remaining pieces of dough, including gathering and rerolling all of the scraps together.

Once all the tortillas have been rolled out and cut, place them one at a time in the center of the hot skillet and cook on one side until bubbles begin to appear on the top surface and the tortilla darkens in color a bit on the underside, about 45 seconds. Flip the tortilla over with a wide spatula, and cook on the other side until more bubbles form and the tortilla darkens on the underside, about another 45 seconds. Remove the tortilla from the pan, place on a moist tea towel, and cover gently. Repeat with the remaining tortillas.

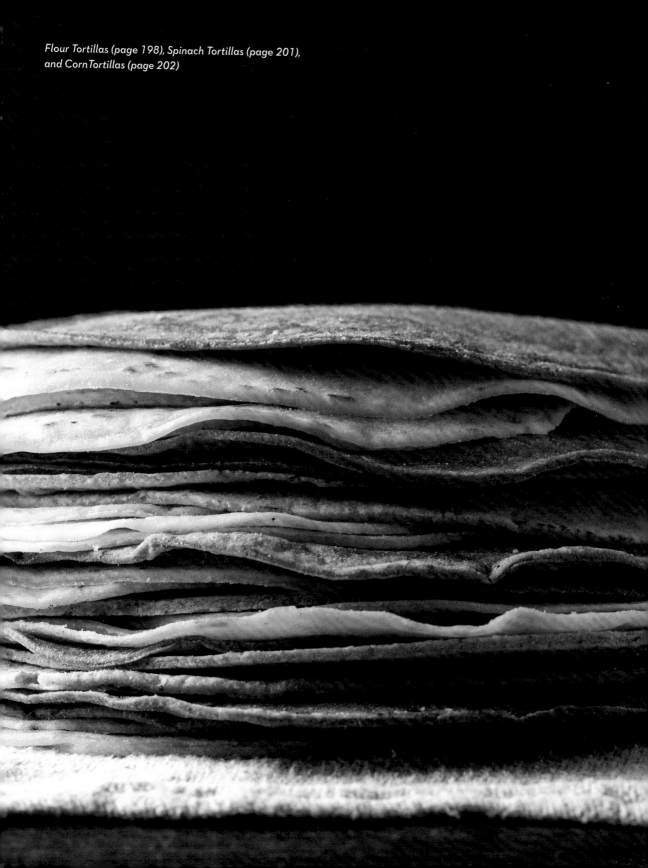

Flour Tortillas (page 198), Spinach Tortillas (page 201), and Corn Tortillas (page 202)

Serving and storage: These tortillas will remain pliable if wrapped in a damp tea towel and then in a sealed plastic bag for a few hours at room temperature. They can be refreshed before eating by searing briefly on both sides in a hot skillet. They can also be cooled completely in a stack, then wrapped tightly in freezer-safe wrap and frozen. Defrost at room temperature and refresh in a hot skillet as described.

spinach tortillas

THESE TORTILLAS DON'T TASTE VERY STRONGLY OF spinach at all, so you can use them in nearly every recipe calling for Flour Tortillas. Packed with the extra nutrients that using a spinach purée in place of water brings, these are versatile and virtuous tortillas!

Place the water in a blender or food processor, followed by the thawed spinach. Purée until very smooth and set aside.

In a large bowl, place the flour, Expandex, baking powder, and salt, and whisk to combine. Add the vegetable shortening and toss it in the dry ingredients. With the tines of a large fork, break up the shortening into small pieces. Create a well in the center of the mixture, and add about ¾ cup of the puréed spinach mixture, and mix to combine. Add more spinach purée by the teaspoonful as necessary to bring the dough together. Press together into a ball, cover with a moist tea towel, and allow to sit for about 20 minutes.

Heat a 10- or 12-inch cast-iron skillet over medium-high heat. Divide the dough into about 8 pieces. Begin with one piece of dough, and cover the rest with a moist tea towel. On a lightly floured surface, with a rolling pin, roll out the first piece of dough about ⅛ inch thick. Cut out a round with an 8-inch metal cake cutter or a similarly sized lid of a pot. Stack the raw tortillas on top of one another, dusting lightly with flour between them, if necessary, to prevent them from sticking. Gather the scraps and set them aside. Repeat with the remaining pieces of dough.

Once all the tortillas have been rolled out and cut, place them one at a time in the center of the hot skillet, and cook on one side until bubbles begin to appear on the top surface and the tortilla darkens in color a bit on the underside, about 45 seconds. Flip and cook on the other side until more bubbles form and the tortilla darkens on the underside, about another 45 seconds. Remove the tortilla from the pan, place on a moist tea towel, and cover gently. Repeat with the remaining tortillas.

Serving and storage: These tortillas will remain pliable if they are wrapped in a damp tea towel and then in a sealed plastic bag for a few hours at room temperature. They can be refreshed before eating by searing briefly on both sides in a hot skillet. They can also be cooled completely in a stack, then wrapped tightly in freezer-safe wrap and frozen. Defrost at room temperature and refresh in a hot skillet as described.

MAKES ABOUT 12 8-INCH
TORTILLAS

¼ cup (2 fluid ounces) warm water

8 ounces frozen spinach, thawed

1¾ cups (245 g) all-purpose gluten-free flour (page 2), plus more for sprinkling

¼ cup (35 g) Expandex modified tapioca starch (page 3) (can be replaced with an equal amount of plain tapioca starch/ flour)

1½ teaspoons baking powder

1 teaspoon (6 g) kosher salt

4½ tablespoons (54 g) vegetable shortening

———————— ⚘ ————————

MAKE-AHEAD OPTION: Spinach tortillas can be made ahead of time, shaped and cooked, then stacked and frozen on a baking sheet unwrapped. Then, wrap them tightly and freeze until ready to use. Defrost at room temperature, and then refresh in a hot, dry skillet, about 30 seconds per side.

———————— ⚘ ————————

corn tortillas

MAKES 10 6-INCH TORTILLAS
OR 5 8-INCH TORTILLAS

2 cups (232 g) gluten-free masa harina
corn flour

¾ teaspoon kosher salt

9 to 11 ounces very warm water (about
90°F)

THESE SIMPLE TORTILLAS ARE MADE WITH ONLY three ingredients—and that's just if you count the salt. Masa harina is made from dried corn that is then cooked in limewater before being dried and ground again; it just smells like corn tortillas—and you'll know it from the moment you open the package. It essentially only needs to be rehydrated before you can cook with it. If it dries out while you're working with it, just work a few drops of water into the dough and begin again. A simple, metal tortilla press is particularly useful in making fresh corn tortillas.

Place the masa and salt in a large bowl, and whisk until well combined. Create a well in the center of the dry ingredients, add 9 ounces water, and mix to combine. The dough should hold together well and have the consistency of Play-Doh: stiff and thick but a bit wet. It will absorb water as it sits. If it is at all dry, add more water, about ½ ounce at a time, until it reaches the proper consistency.

Let the dough rest. Cover the bowl with plastic wrap and allow the dough to sit for 10 to 15 minutes. Remove the plastic wrap and touch the dough. It will have absorbed enough of the water so that it is not crumbly but leaves no residue on your hands when you touch it. Divide the dough into about 10 pieces, and roll each into a tight round between your palms. If the dough is at all crumbly, sprinkle it lightly with some water and knead it into the dough. If using a tortilla press, do not press each piece of dough into a disk with your hands. Line a tortilla press with plastic. (Cut a gallon-size zip-top bag along the sides, and then cut in half into two equal rectangles. Cut off and discard the zip-top and use the two pieces of plastic to line the press.) Then simply press the dough first in the tortilla press. Remove the dough from the press, and roll it out a bit thinner between the two pieces of plastic.

If not using a tortilla press, place one piece of masa dough between two sheets of unbleached parchment paper, and roll into a round about 6 inches in diameter. For a perfect circle, cut a clean round from the dough using a 6-inch cake cutter or lid of a pot of similar diameter. Remove the top sheet of parchment, and peel the bottom sheet of parchment away from the raw tortilla.

Cook the tortillas. Heat a flat cast-iron skillet over medium-high heat until very hot. Place the tortillas, one at a time, in the hot pan. Allow to cook undisturbed until the tortilla begins to pull away from the pan around the edges, about 45 seconds. With a flat, wide spatula, flip the tortilla over, and cook for about 15 seconds. Flip once more, and cook for another 15 seconds. Remove the tortilla from the skillet, and cover with a moist tea towel. Repeat with the remaining dough, gathering and rerolling any scraps and stacking the tortillas under the towel.

Serving and storage: If you don't plan to use the corn tortillas right away, they will remain pliable if stored at room temperature, wrapped in a damp tea towel, for a few hours. They can be refreshed before eating by searing briefly on both sides in a hot skillet. They can also be cooled completely in a stack, then wrapped tightly in freezer-safe wrap and frozen. Defrost at room temperature and refresh in a hot skillet as described.

MAKE-AHEAD OPTION: Corn tortillas can be made ahead of time, shaped and cooked, then stacked on top of one another and frozen on a baking sheet unwrapped. Once the tortillas are completely defrosted, they should be easy to separate from one another. Then, wrap them tightly and freeze until ready to use. Defrost at room temperature, and then refresh in a hot, dry skillet, about 30 seconds per side.

soft tacos

ALMOST EQUAL PARTS FLOUR AND MASA HARINA,
these soft tacos are like a cross between corn and flour tortillas.
They taste and smell like a corn tortilla, but they can be rolled
thinner like a flour tortilla (page 198) and are more versatile and
pliable than a true corn tortilla (page 202). In any recipe that
calls for a soft taco, a similarly sized corn or flour tortilla can be
easily substituted.

...like a flour tortilla (page 198)... a true corn tortilla (page 202)...

1½ cups (210 g) all-purpose gluten-free
   flour (page 2)
1½ cups (174 g) gluten-free masa harina
   corn flour
1 teaspoon kosher salt
1½ teaspoons baking powder
4 tablespoons (48 g) nonhydrogenated
   vegetable shortening
1 cup (8 fluid ounces) iced water (ice cubes
   don't count in the volume measurement), plus more by the ¼ teaspoonful

In a large bowl, place the flour, masa marina, salt, and baking
powder, and whisk to combine. Add the vegetable shortening,
and toss it in the dry ingredients. With the tines of a large fork,
break up the shortening into small pieces about the size of small
peas. Create a well in the center of the mixture, and add about
¾ cup (6 fluid ounces) of the water. Mix to combine. The dough
will come together and be thick. Add as much water as necessary to bring the dough together into a ball. Press together into
a ball, cover with a moist tea towel, and allow to sit for about
20 minutes. The dough will stiffen a bit as it absorbs more of
the water.

Heat a 10- or 12-inch cast-iron skillet over medium-high heat.
Divide the dough into about 10 equal pieces. Begin with one
piece of dough, and cover the rest with a moist tea towel to
prevent them from drying out. On a lightly floured surface, with
a rolling pin, roll out the first piece of dough until it is ⅛ inch
thick. Cut out a round with a 6-inch metal cake cutter or the
lid of a pot. Stack the raw tacos on top of one another, dusting
lightly with flour between them, if necessary, to prevent them
from sticking. Gather the scraps and set them aside. Repeat
with the remaining pieces of dough, gathering and rerolling
all of the scraps together. You should be able to make 2 more
tacos out of the scraps.

Once all the tacos have been rolled out and cut, place them
one at a time in the center of the hot skillet and cook on one
side until bubbles begin to appear on the top surface and the
taco darkens in color a bit on the underside, about 45 seconds.
Flip over with a wide spatula, and cook on the other side until
more bubbles form and the taco darkens on the underside,
about another 45 seconds. Remove from the pan, place on a
moist tea towel, and cover gently.

---❧---

MAKE-AHEAD OPTION: Soft tacos can be made ahead of time, shaped and cooked, then stacked one on top of another and frozen on a baking sheet unwrapped. Then, wrap them tightly and freeze until ready to use. Defrost at room temperature, and then refresh in a hot, dry skillet, about 30 seconds per side. Once the soft tacos are completely defrosted, they should be easy to separate from one another.

---⚘---

Serving and storage: If you don't plan to use the soft tacos right away, they will remain pliable if stored at room temperature, wrapped in a damp tea towel, for a few hours. They can be refreshed before eating by searing briefly on both sides in a hot skillet. They can also be cooled completely in a stack, then wrapped tightly in freezer-safe wrap and frozen. Defrost at room temperature and refresh in a hot skillet as described.

soft tapioca cheese wraps

THESE WONDROUS WRAPS ARE A SPIN OFF OF PÃO de queijo, or Brazilian cheese bread. Soft and incredibly pliable, even when completely cool, they are ideal for handheld dinners and lunch boxes alike. There are a few secrets to success with this recipe: First, use a very good-quality tapioca starch (page 3). Second, let the food processor work long enough to create an emulsion. Finally, if your ingredients are too warm when you transfer them to the food processor, they will not thicken into a dough, and your food processor may overheat and shut down. Don't worry—you didn't burn it out. Let it cool and try again. This is one recipe for which effective dairy-free substitutes are simply not available.

MAKES 10 8-INCH WRAPS

1 cup (8 fluid ounces) milk, divided

2½ cups (300 g) tapioca starch/flour, plus more for sprinkling

¼ teaspoon kosher salt

3 tablespoons (42 g) neutral oil

1 egg (60 g, weighed out of shell), at room temperature, beaten

7 ounces low-moisture part-skim mozzarella cheese, grated

2 ounces Parmigiano-Reggiano cheese, finely grated

In a medium saucepan, bring a scant ¾ cup of the milk to a simmer over medium heat. As soon as the milk begins to simmer, turn off the heat and add the tapioca flour and salt, and then the oil. Mix to combine. The mixture will look curdled and will be difficult to bring together. Allow the dough to cool for at least 10 minutes, or until it is no longer hot to the touch. Place the beaten egg and the cheeses in the bowl of a food processor fitted with a steel blade, and then add the cooled tapioca mixture. Pulse a few times to smooth out the dough, then turn the food processor on high until the dough is very smooth (at least 2 minutes). The dough will be sticky but will become less sticky as it cools. If the dough seems too thick, add more milk, about a tablespoon at a time, and process again until smooth. Use a wet spatula to remove it from the food processor. With wet hands or kitchen tools, divide the dough into two equal pieces and wrap each tightly in plastic wrap. Place it in the freezer to chill for at least 30 minutes or in the refrigerator for 2 hours or up to overnight.

Once the dough has chilled, heat a 10-inch cast-iron skillet over medium heat (or a nonstick skillet over low heat). Unwrap one chilled piece of dough and place on a flat surface lightly sprinkled with tapioca flour. With a sharp knife or bench or bowl scraper, divide the dough into 10 equal pieces, each about 3 ounces. Dust each piece generously with tapioca flour, and roll

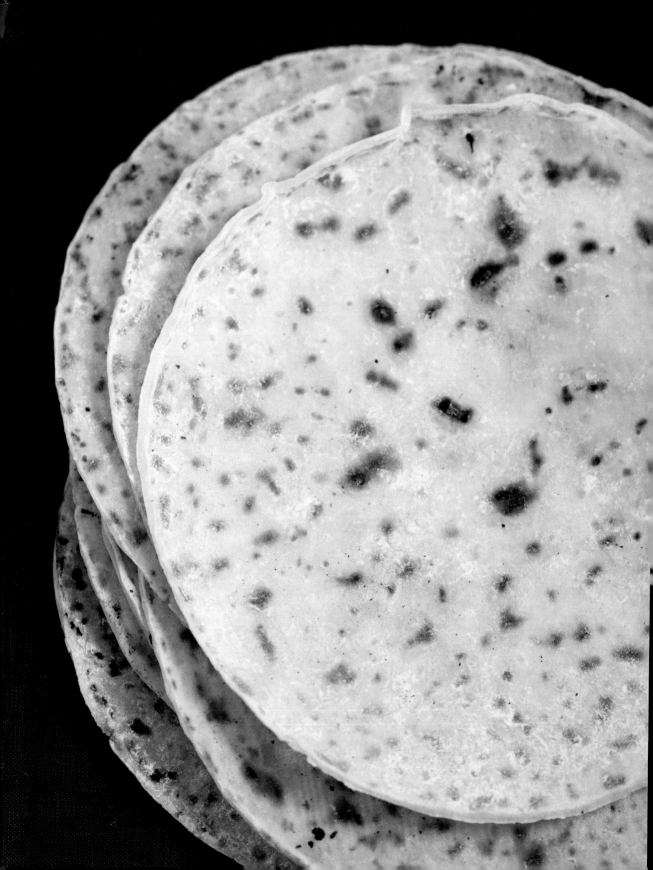

out into a circle 8 inches in diameter, moving the dough often and sprinkling it with tapioca flour when necessary to prevent it from sticking.

Carefully place the first circle of dough onto the hot skillet and allow it to cook until the underside is cooked and the wrap can be lifted easily with a wide spatula, about 1 minute. Flip the wrap over and press down evenly with the spatula to sear the other side. Cook until the underside is set, about another 40 seconds. Remove from the skillet and cover with a moist tea towel. Repeat with the remaining 4 pieces of dough, and then with the other half of dough.

Serving and storage: If you don't plan to use the wraps right away, they will remain pliable if stored at room temperature, wrapped in a damp tea towel, for a few hours. They can be refreshed before eating by searing briefly on both sides in a hot skillet. They can also be cooled completely in a stack, then wrapped tightly in freezer-safe wrap and frozen. Defrost at room temperature and refresh in a hot skillet as described.

MAKE-AHEAD OPTION: Soft tapioca wraps can be made ahead of time, shaped and cooked, then stacked one on top of another and frozen on a baking sheet unwrapped. Then, wrap them tightly and freeze until ready to use. Defrost at room temperature, and then refresh in a hot, dry skillet, about 30 seconds per side. Once the wraps are completely defrosted, they should be easy to separate from one another.

naan bread

MAKES 8 PIECES

2½ cups (350 g) Gluten-Free Bread Flour
(page 4), plus more for sprinkling
1⅔ teaspoons (5 g) instant yeast
1½ tablespoons (18 g) sugar
¼ teaspoon cream of tartar
½ teaspoon (3 g) kosher salt
⅓ cup plain yogurt, at room temperature
3 tablespoons (42 g) ghee or unsalted
butter, melted and cooled
¾ cup plus 2 tablespoons warm water
(about 95°F)
Ghee or unsalted butter, for frying

*PILLOW-SOFT, LIGHTLY FRIED NAAN BREAD IS
slightly crispy on the outside, fluffy on the inside. It's not a
traditional bread to serve as the base for any of the wraps and
roll-ups in Chapter 5, but its slightly tangy taste and delightful
texture are very well suited to many of them, most notably the
Chicken Gyros.*

In the bowl of your stand mixer, place the flour, yeast, sugar, and
cream of tartar, and use a handheld whisk to combine well. Add
the salt, and whisk to combine. Add the yogurt, ghee, and water,
and knead on low speed with the dough hook until combined.
Raise the mixer speed to medium high, and knead until smooth,
about 5 minutes. Spray a silicone spatula lightly with cooking
oil spray, and scrape down the sides of the bowl. Transfer the
dough to a lightly oiled bowl or proofing bucket large enough
for the dough to rise to double its size, and cover with an oiled
piece of plastic wrap (or the oiled top to your proofing bucket).
Place the dough in a warm, draft-free location to rise until
nearly doubled in size, about 1½ hours. Place the dough in the
refrigerator for at least 30 minutes to chill before handling.

Line a rimmed baking sheet with unbleached parchment
paper, spray the paper lightly with cooking oil, and set it aside.
Remove the dough from the refrigerator, and turn it out onto a
lightly floured surface. Sprinkle lightly with extra flour, and turn
the dough over on itself using a bench or bowl scraper. Sprinkle
again very lightly with flour, and continue to fold the dough over
on itself to knead it lightly until it's smoother. Using the bench
or bowl scraper, divide the dough in half, then each half in half,
until you have 8 pieces, each about 95 grams. Shape the first
piece of dough. Cover the remaining pieces of dough with a
moist tea towel so that they don't dry out. Flouring the surface
as necessary to keep the dough from sticking, use a rolling pin
to roll each piece of dough into an elongated oval about ⅜ inch
thick. Repeat with the remaining pieces of dough. Place each
piece of shaped dough 2 inches apart from one another on the
prepared baking sheet. Cover with lightly oiled plastic wrap,
and set in a warm, draft-free location to rise until nearly doubled
in size, about 1 hour.

As the dough is nearing the end of its rise, place about 2
tablespoons of ghee in a cast-iron skillet and melt over medium-
high heat. Once the pan is hot, place the first piece of dough

──────── ☙ ────────

MAKE-AHEAD OPTION: The raw dough can be made up to 3 days ahead of time, placed in a sealed proofing container and placed in the refrigerator for its first rise. The raw dough should not be frozen. The bread is best made on the day it is to be eaten, then wrapped in a moist towel and kept at room temperature until ready to serve.

──────── ❧ ────────

in the pan. Fry on one side until large bubbles begin to form, about 1 minute. Continue to fry for another 30 seconds to 1 minute, or until the underside is golden brown. Flip the bread to cook on the other side until browned, another minute or so. Transfer to a paper towel. Repeat with the remaining seven pieces of dough. Serve immediately.

pretzel dough

PRETZEL DOUGH IS THE SMOOTH, EASY-TO-HANDLE enriched dough that is essential to making Pretzel Dogs (page 51), but it can also be used to twist into soft pretzel shapes or make into rolls.

In the bowl of your stand mixer, place the flour, dry milk, yeast, cream of tartar, and brown sugar, and use a handheld whisk to combine well, breaking up any lumps in the brown sugar. Add the salt, and whisk to combine. Add the butter and water, and mix on low speed with the dough hook until combined. Raise the mixer speed to medium and knead for about 5 minutes. The dough will be sticky but smooth and stretchy. Spray a silicone spatula lightly with cooking oil spray, and use it to scrape down the sides of the bowl. Transfer the dough to a lightly oiled bowl or proofing bucket large enough for it to rise to double its size, spray the top of the dough with cooking oil spray, and cover with a piece of oiled plastic wrap or the oiled top of your proofing bucket. Place the dough in a warm, draft-free location to rise to about double its size, about 1½ hours. Place the risen dough in the refrigerator to chill for about 30 minutes to make handling the dough much easier, or skip the initial rise in a warm, draft-free environment and allow the dough to rise in the refrigerator until nearly doubled, up to 3 days before using in a recipe. Work with the dough cold when shaping it for use in the appropriate recipe.

MAKES ABOUT 3 POUNDS

3¼ cups (455 g) Gluten-Free Bread Flour (page 4)

²⁄₃ cup (40 g) nonfat dry milk, ground finely

2 teaspoons (6 g) instant yeast

¼ teaspoon cream of tartar

1 tablespoon (14 g) packed light-brown sugar

1 teaspoon (6 g) kosher salt

4 tablespoons (56 g) unsalted butter, at room temperature

1¼ cups plus 2 tablespoons (11 fluid ounces) warm water (about 95°F)

MAKE-AHEAD OPTION: The raw dough can be made up to 3 days ahead of time, placed in a sealed proofing container, and placed in the refrigerator for its first rise. The raw dough should not be frozen.

thin crust pizza dough

FOR THE STARTER

1½ cups (210 g) Gluten-Free Bread Flour
(page 4)
2⅓ teaspoons (7 g) instant yeast
2¼ teaspoons (9 g) granulated sugar
1½ cups (12 fluid ounces) warm water
(about 95°F)

FOR THE DOUGH

3 cups (420 g) Gluten-Free Bread Flour
(page 4), plus more for sprinkling
1 tablespoon (18 g) kosher salt
Starter

———————— ⚜ ————————

MAKE-AHEAD OPTION: The raw dough
can be made up to 5 days ahead of time,
placed in a sealed proofing container, and
placed in the refrigerator for its first rise.
The raw dough should not be frozen.

———————— ⚜ ————————

*ALTHOUGH FLUFFIER, THICK CRUST DOUGH IS IDEAL
for baking a pizza you can sink your teeth into, thin crust pizza
dough is ideal for shaping into everything from Beef Stromboli and Garlic Pizza Breadsticks (pages 120 and 84) to Pigs
in Blankets (page 47), Pizza Bites, and Pizza Pinwheels (pages
87 and 88). As it rises, it becomes easier to handle and more
flavorful as the yeast develops. If you don't like a very yeasty
flavor in your pizza crust but you want dough that is simple to
handle, allow it to rise in the refrigerator in a tightly sealed proofing bucket for no more than 2 days, and always work with cold
dough.*

To make the starter, place all of the starter ingredients in a
medium-size bowl, and whisk until well combined. The mixture will be thick and shapeless. Cover and set the bowl aside
in a warm, draft-free location to rise until doubled, about
45 minutes.

Once the starter has finished rising, make the dough. Place
the flour and salt in the bowl of your stand mixer, and use a
handheld whisk to combine well. Add the risen starter to the
bowl, and mix on low speed with the dough hook until combined. Raise the mixer speed to medium and knead for about
5 minutes. The dough will begin as a rough ball and will become
very sticky and rather stiff but still stretchy and smooth.

Spray a silicone spatula lightly with cooking oil spray, and
use it to scrape down the sides of the bowl. Transfer the dough
to a lightly oiled bowl or proofing bucket large enough for
it to rise to double its size, spray the top of the dough with
cooking oil spray, and cover with a piece of oiled plastic wrap
or the oiled top of your proofing bucket. Place the dough in a
warm, draft-free location to rise to about double its size, about
1½ hours. Place the risen dough in the refrigerator to chill for
about 30 minutes to make handling the dough much easier, or
skip the initial rise in a warm, draft-free environment and allow
the dough to rise in the refrigerator until nearly doubled, up
to 3 days before using in a recipe. Work with the dough cold
when shaping it for use in the appropriate recipe.

yeast-free pizza dough

LET'S BE REAL: SOMETIMES YOU DON'T PLAN AHEAD. Maybe you thought you had a batch of yeasted pizza dough rising away in the refrigerator, only to open up the refrigerator door and find it nowhere in sight. Maybe you just forgot that everyone would be hungry again. Hey, it happens. For those moments, you need this recipe. To make it easier to handle, do place it in the refrigerator to chill for a few minutes. And double the recipe if you plan to use it in any of the recipes that call for the Thin Crust Pizza Dough (page 214) in this book, as this recipe makes 1½ pounds of dough to that recipe's 3 pounds.

In the bowl of a stand mixer fitted with the dough hook, place the flour, baking powder, and salt, and whisk to combine well with a separate handheld whisk. Add the olive oil, honey, and water, and mix on low speed with the dough hook until combined. Raise the mixer speed to medium and knead for about 5 minutes. The dough will begin as a rough ball and become very sticky but should be smooth and somewhat stretchy. Spray a silicone spatula lightly with cooking oil spray, and scrape down the sides of the bowl. Transfer the dough to a lightly oiled bowl or proofing bucket, and cover with an oiled piece of plastic wrap (or the oiled top to your proofing bucket) and place in the refrigerator to chill for at least 10 minutes to make it easier to handle. Work with the dough cold when shaping it for use in the appropriate recipe.

MAKES ABOUT 1½ POUNDS

3 cups (420 g) Gluten-Free Bread Flour (page 4), plus more for sprinkling
4½ teaspoons baking powder
1 teaspoon kosher salt
2 tablespoons (28 g) extra-virgin olive oil
1 tablespoon (21 g) honey
1 cup (8 fluid ounces) lukewarm water

panko-style breadcrumbs

MAKES ABOUT 3 CUPS

4 to 5 medium slices gluten-free bread, roughly torn

½ teaspoon kosher salt

PANKO-STYLE BREADCRUMBS HAVE A LARGER GRAIN than the fine breadcrumbs that at least used to be most common. They're ideal for frying, as they absorb less oil than traditional breadcrumbs. They can be purchased ready-made (my favorite brand is Ian's), but they're really quite expensive and typically need to be ordered online. In a pinch, try pulsing the simplest gluten-free corn flakes (try Erewhon brand, which have no sugar) in a food processor until they're the proper size and consistency. Or save those odds and ends from a loaf of gluten-free bread and make your own panko-style breadcrumbs once your stash reaches critical mass.

Preheat your oven to 325°F. Line a large rimmed baking sheet with aluminum foil and set it aside.

In the bowl of a food processor fitted with a steel blade, place the torn bread and salt. Cover the food processor and pulse until coarse crumbs form. Transfer the breadcrumbs to the prepared baking sheet and spread them into an even layer.

Place the baking sheet in the center of the preheated oven and bake for about 8 minutes. Remove the breadcrumbs from the oven and stir to redistribute. Return to the oven and bake until lightly golden brown all over, about another 7 minutes. Remove from the oven and allow to cool completely on the baking sheet before transferring to a freezer-safe container. Seal tightly and place in the refrigerator or freezer until ready to use.

The breadcrumbs can be used directly from the refrigerator or freezer, without defrosting. They will keep for months in the freezer.

metric conversion chart

The recipes in this book have not been tested with metric measurements, so some variations might occur. Remember that the weight of dry ingredients varies according to the volume or density factor: 1 cup of flour weighs far less than 1 cup of sugar, and 1 tablespoon doesn't necessarily hold 3 teaspoons.

GENERAL FORMULA FOR METRIC CONVERSION

Ounces to grams	multiply ounces by 28.35
Grams to ounces	multiply grams by 0.035
Pounds to grams	multiply pounds by 453.5
Pounds to kilograms	multiply pounds by 0.45
Cups to liters	multiply cups by 0.24
Fahrenheit to Celsius	subtract 32 from Fahrenheit temperature, multiply by 5, divide by 9
Celsius to Fahrenheit	multiply Celsius temperature by 9, divide by 5, add 32

VOLUME (LIQUID) MEASUREMENTS

1 teaspoon	= 1/6 fluid ounce	= 5 milliliters
1 tablespoon	= 1/2 fluid ounce	= 15 milliliters
2 tablespoons	= 1 fluid ounce	= 30 milliliters
1/4 cup	= 2 fluid ounces	= 60 milliliters
1/3 cup	= 2 2/3 fluid ounces	= 79 milliliters
1/2 cup	= 4 fluid ounces	= 118 milliliters
1 cup or 1/2 pint	= 8 fluid ounces	= 250 milliliters
2 cups or 1 pint	= 16 fluid ounces	= 500 milliliters
4 cups or 1 quart	= 32 fluid ounces	= 1,000 milliliters
1 gallon	= 4 liters	

WEIGHT (MASS) MEASUREMENTS

1 ounce	= 30 grams	
2 ounces	= 55 grams	
3 ounces	= 85 grams	
4 ounces	= 1/4 pound	= 125 grams
8 ounces	= 1/2 pound	= 240 grams
12 ounces	= 3/4 pound	= 375 grams
16 ounces	= 1 pound	= 454 grams

OVEN TEMPERATURE EQUIVALENTS, FAHRENHEIT (F) AND CELSIUS (C)

100°F	= 38°C
200°F	= 95°C
250°F	= 120°C
300°F	= 150°C
350°F	= 180°C
400°F	= 205°C
450°F	= 230°C

VOLUME (DRY) MEASUREMENTS

1/4 teaspoon	= 1 milliliter
1/2 teaspoon	= 2 milliliters
3/4 teaspoon	= 4 milliliters
1 teaspoon	= 5 milliliters
1 tablespoon	= 15 milliliters
1/4 cup	= 59 milliliters
1/3 cup	= 79 milliliters
1/2 cup	= 118 milliliters
2/3 cup	= 158 milliliters
3/4 cup	= 177 milliliters
1 cup	= 225 milliliters
4 cups or 1 quart	= 1 liter
1/2 gallon	= 2 liters
1 gallon	= 4 liters

LINEAR MEASUREMENTS

1/2 inch	= 1 1/2 cm
1 inch	= 2 1/2 cm
6 inches	= 15 cm
8 inches	= 20 cm
10 inches	= 25 cm
12 inches	= 30 cm
20 inches	= 50 cm

acknowledgments

I don't talk about my family very much on my blog, and I don't include photos of them in my cookbooks. But behind every recipe, behind every photo, there they are. I mean, literally, they're probably right there. Waiting to eat. But they're also there figuratively, celebrating each recipe failure, since they know I'll make it again and again, and they'll get to eat it as many times. They're there, finding ways to work "my mom's a cookbook author" into casual conversation with their friends' parents, their coaches, and their teachers. So to my children, Bailey, Jonathan, and Ava, your enthusiasm fuels me. Thank you for that. And to my husband, Brian, my confidence may ebb and flow, but yours in me never, ever does. That means more to me than you know.

To my agent, Brandi Bowles, thank you for being ever the voice of reason and for driving a hard bargain—on both sides. I love, and depend upon, having you on my side.

To my editor extraordinaire, Renée Sedliar, I'm as grateful as ever for both your line edits and your big picture understanding and knowledge. I take my cue from you. When you're confident in our product, then so am I.

To Jennifer May, for photographs that quite literally take my breath away. Your easy but intense manner on set is something I don't think I'll ever forget.

To Erin McDowell, for making the pastry perfect (how do you *do* that?) and the shoot run smoothly on pace and at perfect pitch. To Sarah Daniels (aka Honey), for frying with two hands when necessary and appropriate.

To Amber Morris and the rest of the production team at Perseus Books Group, you always strike the right balance between respecting my experience and reminding me of my role in the process.

To Alex Camlin and the rest of the design team, once again, you have done Jen's photos justice, both on the cover and in the book's interior. You really are the very best.

And to my blog readers, thank you for being my coworkers and cheerleaders. And thank you for understanding the value of a cookbook, even in the Internet age. Much love and gratitude to you all.

index

Note: Page references in *italics* indicate photographs.

about the author

Nicole Hunn is the personality behind the popular *Gluten-Free on a Shoestring* blog and book series. She has been featured in high-profile national print and broadcast outlets, including the *New York Times*, *Parade* magazine, *Better Homes and Gardens*, *Parents* magazine, Epicurious.com, ABC News, *The Better Show*, and many others. Nicole has also been a contributing gluten-free expert for SheKnows.com Food and *Living Without* and *Gluten-Free Living* magazines. She lives in Westchester County, New York, with her husband and three children. For more information and recipes, please visit www.glutenfreeonashoestring.com.